Attacking Soccer
Mastering the Modern Game

For reasons of better readability, we have decided to use the male (neutral) form of address throughout the book, which of course also includes the female form.

Peter Schreiner & Norbert Elgert

# Attacking Soccer

## Mastering the Modern Game

Meyer & Meyer Sport

Original title: Moderner Angriffsfußball
Aachen: Meyer & Meyer, © 2012
Translated by: AAA Translation®, USA

British Library Cataloguing in Publication Data
A catalogue record for this book is available from the British Library

**Attacking Soccer**
**Mastering the Modern Game**
Peter Schreiner, Norbert Elgert
Maidenhead: Meyer & Meyer Sport (UK) Ltd., 2013
ISBN: 978-1-78255-008-2

© 2013 by Meyer & Meyer Sport (UK) Ltd.
Auckland, Beirut, Budapest, Cairo, Cape Town, Dubai, Hägendorf,
Indianapolis, Maidenhead, Singapore, Sydney, Tehran, Wien
Member of the World
Sport Publishers' Association (WSPA)
www.w-s-p-a.org
Printed by: B.O.S.S Druck und Medien GmbH
ISBN: 978-1-78255-008-2
E-Mail: info@m-m-sports.com
www.m-m-sports.com

# Contents

## Thank you

We would like to thank Horst Wein, whose workshops and books provided us with valuable suggestions.

We would also like to thank Marion Becker who, on demand, continuously created new players and tools for the easy Sports-Graphics software, allowing us to provide realistic illustrations of our forms of training.

Special thanks to Conny Elgert, for her energetic and inspiring support during the creation of this book!

## Preface

Soccer fans all over the world love attacking soccer with its quick combinations, spectacular dribbling, and beautiful goals. Top teams like Real Madrid, Arsenal London, and Bayern Munich demonstrate how modern and successful soccer is played. All players immediately switch to offense after they gain possession of the ball. They do not wait until the opponent has gotten organized but quickly utilize holes in the opposing defense. They penetrate the opponent's penalty area with very few, mostly direct plays.

After gaining possession of the ball, it is crucial to quickly mount a counter attack while the opposing line is still disorganized and open. If the opponent quickly reorganizes and switches to defense, it is best to launch a possession attack.

Counter attacks and possession attacks are two of the three main themes in this book. But what good are counter attacks and possession attacks without the finish? In Chapter 5 of this book, we will therefore focus extensively on the successful finish, the high point and objective of all attack efforts.

But first a few tips:

- Drills and plays aren't what help your players improve, but rather how the players use them.
- How do you motivate your players? Do you encourage and compliment your players?
- How do you correct your players? What are your areas of emphasis?
- The sections on tips and suggestions are particularly important.

This book provides a systematic compilation of drills.
First, the theoretic aspects of each topic are covered extensively to lay the foundation for the subsequent practical segment. In the practical segment, you will find complex passing and dribbling drills. We recommend these for the second warm-up phase of training, which prepares your players for the main part of training.

All drills and plays have been tested and tried on different age groups and ability levels.

# Legend

## Actions and markings

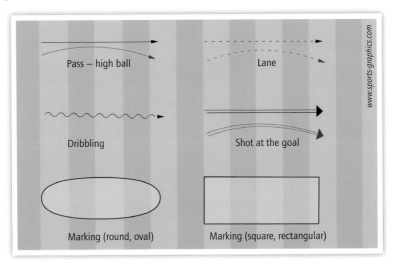

## People (players, goalkeepers, trainer)

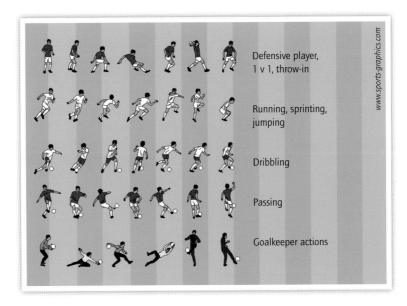

*The illustrations in this book are created with easy Sports-Graphics (www.easy-sports-software.com/)*

# I  *Counter attack*

## 1  Introduction

In today's soccer, the amount of space around the ball is becoming increasingly smaller, but the pressure on the player in possession of the ball from opponent and pressure of time continue to increase. In addition, modern, ball-oriented approaches to defense and strategies make successful actions in the orderly, safe structure of the possession attack more difficult. This fact warrants the development of offensive counter strategies.

This makes the quick counter move after winning the ball all the more important. Many of the goals scored during a game come after a quick touch directly after the ball is won. It is no coincidence that most of the goals in a game are scored after fewer than five passes.

Successful teams switch from defense to offense at lightning speed. In fact, the entire team should mentally prepare for their possible counter attack during the defensive phase. Immediately after gaining possession, the players purposefully utilize the opponent's brief disorganization (ideally as a majority). They don't waste time looking for the quickest, most direct path to the opposing goal.

Successful counter attacks require meticulous and thorough preparation and development during training. There is an important and crucial difference between counter attack and attacking play, or rather attack tactic. Pure attacking play as a team tactic is characterized by the entire team retreating completely into their half when the opponent has possession of the ball and, after regaining possession, starting quick, targeted counter attacks against the opponent, who has moved well up the field and whose defense is thus open.

After gaining possession of the ball, the counter attack produces a quick gain of space and a majority with few passes or high-speed dribbling. Ideally, the first or second pass reaches a teammate in front of the ball.

## 1.1  Counter attack mentality

During the game, all players closely watch the opponent's defense so they can offer a coordinated and appropriate reaction. They read the opponent's game independently but also view it through the same eyes.

A counter attack is always preceded by a mistake by the opponent. The idea is to provoke this mistake. Teams with a counter attack mentality always anticipate the possibility of a counter attack and are prepared to quickly switch to attack mode after gaining possession of the ball. All players keep constant track of the game and know the exact location of ball, opponent, and teammates.

## 1.2    Three counter attack phases

First phase          —          before gaining possession of the ball (preparation).
Second phase      —          after gaining possession of the ball (execution).
Third phase         —          after the counter attack (switch to attack or counter attack by the opponent).

## 1.2.1  Phase prior to gaining possession of the ball

The defending team directs the opponent's attack into a specific zone on the field. The sideline is very helpful for this purpose. Where the opponent's attack is directed depends upon:

- a team's tactics and its own game plan
- the particular game situation
- the opponent's strengths and weaknesses.

The defending team seeks to have a majority at the place where it plans to take possession. The players in front of the ball, usually the forwards, narrow their push toward the ball and, thinking ahead, already stagger themselves smartly toward the depth of the field for a possible counter attack.

To take possession, 2-3 players put well-timed and aggressive pressure on the player on the ball. The best time to do this is when the ball is still on its way to him.

Possible passing lanes to the opposing players near the ball are blocked and players farther away from the ball also push toward the ball. This severely restricts the playing area.

Set pieces are ideal for counter attacks. They should be executed quickly, particularly in the mid-field and in the opposing third, especially if the opponent is still "napping." Opposing set pieces (corners, free kick-centering, and centering) can also be easily used for a quick counter attack. When the goalkeeper intercepts the ball, he initiates a quick counter attack with a throw or punt.

## 1.2.2   Phase after gaining possession of the ball

First, the possession must be secured by dribbling to an unmanned area or by making a pass to a better-positioned teammate. For safety, the player who won possession ideally dribbles or passes the ball immediately to the desired depth. All players already develop their depth of focus before gaining possession and take their first look down field at the latest when they gain possession of the ball.

Next, in order to make a quick decision to counter attack, a reliable technical execution is absolutely necessary. The objective of the counter attack is to score a goal via high-speed dribbling and/or few and quick passes. Low passes are especially well suited because they reach their destination more quickly and are easier to control. Ideal passes are perfectly timed through passes.

The players in front of the ball make well-coordinated runs down the field to get open (caution: off sides!) and offer the player in possession many passing options.

Backs are also encouraged to participate in the counter attack.
A majority should be sought during a counter attack.

There should be no more than one turnover, otherwise the opponent will have plenty of time to reorganize his defense.

A counter attack often ends with a direct shot on the goal. Direct shots on the goal after a pass and at a high rate of speed should therefore be trained more frequently. Players should look for the second chance for a shot at the goal, similar to the rebound in basketball. This, too, should be practiced more in training. During the counter attack, the team must remain tight. Therefore, enough players should stay behind the ball to prevent a dangerous return counter attack.

## 1.2.3   During the opponent's counter attack

The opposing team's ball-winning player must be immediately challenged and kept from initiating a return counter attack. The players who are positioned closest to the player in possession of the ball do this. They prevent a fast dribble, a pass to a near-by player, and especially a long pass. This requires players to anticipate the actions of opposing players (mentally preempt), to coach one another, and to block any possible passing and running lanes.

All other players participating in the counter attack run back behind the ball as fast as possible and, together with the players who remained behind the ball, organize a tight defensive formation. In doing so, they apply the shortest path principle to save strength and energy and more quickly reoccupy all positions.

# 2    Prerequisites for a successful counter attack

## Technical prerequisites

- mastery of all 1 v 1 and tackling techniques
- the ability to successfully play offensive and defensive 1 v 1
- the ability to dribble at a high rate of speed and to move the ball down the field
- the ability to pass quickly, accurately and powerfully to a teammate and into his running path
- the ability to make technically clean, controlled through passes at fastest running speed
- exceptional scoring technique with any part of the foot, especially full instep, outside and inside foot, inside toe
- the ability to successfully finish with a volley, such as hip-turn kick, header, etc.
- the ability to successfully rebound

## Tactical prerequisites

- a good grasp of game and tactics
- playing intelligence
- the ability to accurately read a game (independently and together)
- the ability to anticipate well and quickly
- playing and action speed
- the ability to direct/steer the opponent's game into specific zones based on mutual soccer concepts, plans, and perceptions
- the ability to effectively play the pressing game
- the ability of all players to run intelligently and in a coordinated manner during counter attacks and before a shot at the goal
- mastery of the off-sides rule
- mastery of individual, group and team tactics with respect to offensive and defensive principles

## Physical prerequisites

- speed with and without the ball
- a good foundation and competition-specific endurance to be able to successfully counter attack even in the last few minutes
- strength and assertiveness to be able to persevere when fighting for the ball 1 v 1

## Mental prerequisites

- courage to take risks
- self-control, risk assessment
- self-confidence
- assertiveness
- resilience
- positive aggressiveness
- collaborative counter attack mentality
- strong desire to win

## Social prerequisites

- team player
- cooperativeness
- sense of responsibility

## 2.1    Systematic teaching and training of the counter attack

It is very important that you systematically teach your players the theoretical and practical aspects of the counter attack from the very beginning. Methodic-didactic principles should be taken into consideration when teaching the counter attack:

- from easy to difficult
- from the familiar to the unfamiliar
- from the simple to the complex

Training points of emphasis when teaching the counter attack are:
- winning the ball
- lightning-fast changeover from defense to offense
- preparation of a possible shot at the goal
- the shot at the goal
- behavior after the counter attack

## 2.2 Preliminary practice to counter attack – Playing down the field

### Progression

This is a drill for playing down the field. The starting player A skips over a row (or a player – here: C) and plays to B (1). B lets the ball bounce to C (2). C plays to D and takes the position of B (3). B plays a wall pass with D (4, 5) and takes the position of D. D settles the ball and dribbles to position A (6). The drill is then continued on the other side via E.

### Variation

- Simultaneous start on both sides to the left and right. Here, it is advisable to use two start cones for A and E.

### Tips and suggestions

- Each player keeps moving to the next station.
- C advances during the initial pass and challenges A for the ball. But A plays to B and skips C.
- Use body feints.

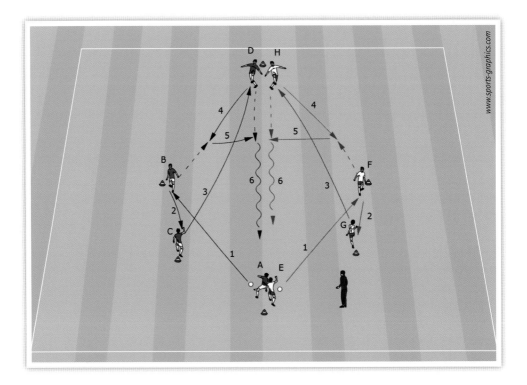

## 2.3    From 1 v 0 to 3 v 2 + 1 (by Horst Wein)

A counter attack places high demand on the players' perception and decisiveness. The positions of teammates and opponents change at a furious pace. The ideal opportunity is easily blown. Often a complex situation changes within a fraction of a second and a new decision is necessary. A possible pass is no longer expedient; a fast dribble to the goal is no longer possible because the zone has been blocked. The players always have multiple options.

The following method begins with simple tasks, which gradually become more complex. From a counter attack scenario without opposing player on one goal with a keeper, we will develop counter attack scenarios with a constantly increasing number of players that start with small contests.

Depending on the behavior of the defensive and offensive players and the overall situation, the attacking players make decisions aimed at utilizing a majority and very quickly finding a scoring opportunity. The timing of the shot at the goal must be such that the shooter can control the shot at a run without delay.

# 1 v 0

## Progression

A forward (A) starts a fast dribble at the centerline and finishes as fast as possible with a shot at the goal.

## Competitions

- Timed competition without goalkeeper – a goal is only valid when the player takes a shot at the goal from the penalty box.
- Timed competition with neutral goalkeeper in a large goal.
- Two players simultaneously run at two (or three) mini goals.
- Two players simultaneously run at two large goals with goalkeeper.

## Variation

- The players (B) start from different positions at the centerline.

## Tips and suggestions

- Dribbling to the shooting position as fast as possible (speed dribbling with as few touches as possible).
- Looking for the most direct path to the goal.
- Technical execution cannot be adversely affected by speed.
- Competitions create time pressure.

# 1 v 0 + 1 opponent from behind

## Progression

One forward starts with a fast dribble. As soon as the player moves the ball forward with the first touch, an opposing player starts from a "fair" distance (about 7 feet).

## Competitions

- 1 v 1 contest: Players alternate three attacks each. Who successfully finishes the most attacks?
- Group competition with an empty goal: A scored goal is only valid beyond a predetermined line.
- Group competition with two goals with a goalkeeper from the opposite team.

## Variation

- The starting points change (start from the center, left or right from the outside).

## Tips and suggestions

- At the right moment, the dribbler crosses the running path of the player who is attacking from behind, especially if the pursuer is very fast.
- Watch the goalkeeper's demeanor.
- Do not play the ball too far forward.

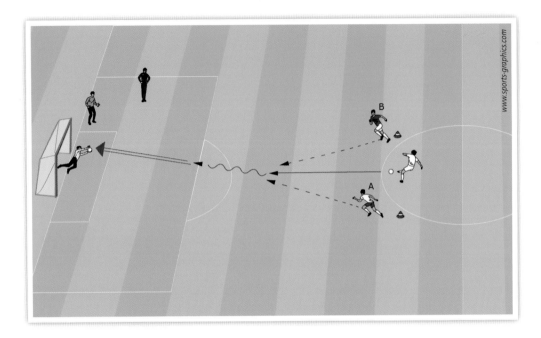

## Sprint duel for the long pass

### Progression

Two players run from the centerline for a steep pass played fairly into the zone by a passing player. Whoever wins the race becomes the offensive player, the other plays defense.

### Variations

- Starters run to the stationary ball positioned approximately 20-25 yards from the goal. The trainer gives an audible or visual signal.
- The passing player is behind the sprinters and is not visible (reaction training).
- The passing player is in a dribble zone (e.g., in the center circle) and makes a pass from a dribble into the zone. This improves the ability to anticipate a pass based on the dribbler's movements.

### Tips and suggestions

- Crossing over into the running path of the opponent during a sprint can also decide the race for the ball.
- Allow for sufficient recovery time.

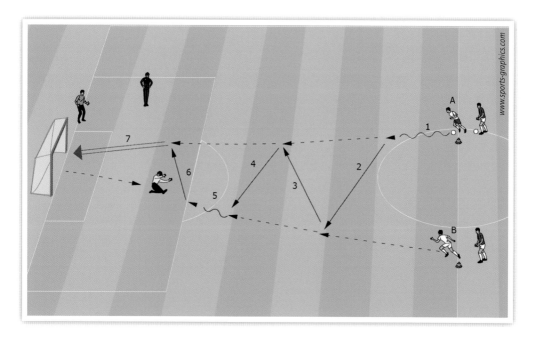

# Counter attack 2 v 0

## Progression (preliminary exercise)

Two players (A and B) run as fast as possible from the centerline to take a shot at the goal in the penalty box. They must play at least two passes.

## Competitions

- Which pair is the quickest to score a valid goal in the penalty box without a goalkeeper?
- Same progression with a goalkeeper.
- Contest at two goals with two goalkeepers as a team competition.
- The goalkeeper is from the opposing team.
- A defensive player attacks from a position behind the pairs' starting point.

## Variation

- Contest at two goals. Pairs from two teams play against each other.

## Tips and suggestions

- It is important that the players cover the space as fast as possible. This only happens if they play very few passes and don't dribble too long.
- Counter attack – quick and successful: A plays a through pass to B, who challenges the goalkeeper and plays a through pass to A, who finishes with a shot at the goal.

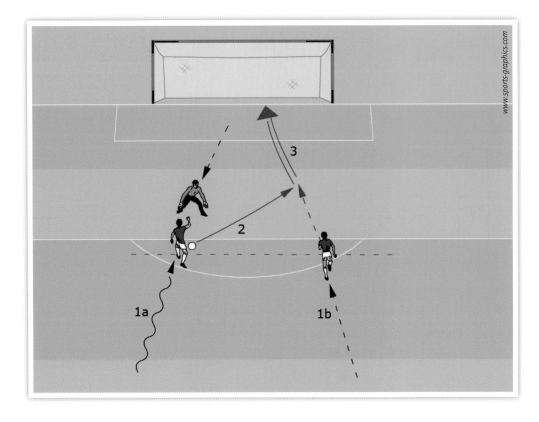

## How to play 2 v 0 against a goalkeeper

1a and 1b should be far enough apart (at least 8-10 yards) for the final pass.

The final pass past the goalkeeper should be played outside the goalkeeper's range. The overall attack behavior depends on the goalkeeper's demeanor.

- How does the goalkeeper attack?
- How does he behave in the zone?
- Does he delay and wait for the attacker to make a mistake?

The goalkeeper advances and tries to steal the ball from 1a. 1b has also run and stays behind the ball to avoid going offside. Player 1a plays a through pass to 1b out of the goalkeeper's range, and 1b has no problem putting the ball into the empty goal.

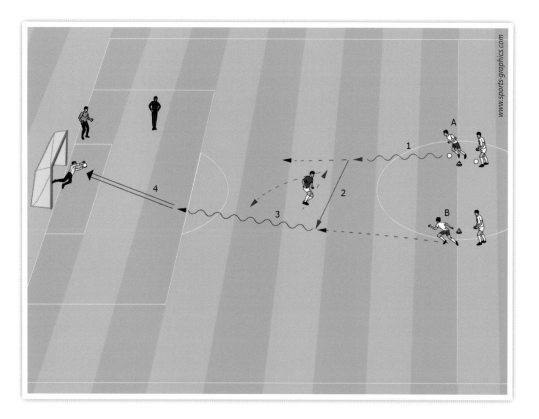

## 2 v 1

### Progression

Two offensive players try to outplay one defender at a high rate of speed. A fast dribble and shot on the large goal with goalkeeper follow the pass past the opponent.

### Tips and suggestions

- The starting player estimates the distance and decides if he is fast enough to dribble toward the defender, challenge him, and then outplay him with a through pass to his partner.
- If the distance to the opponent is very long, the starting player begins with a through pass to his partner, who then challenges the opponent.
- Set a time limit.

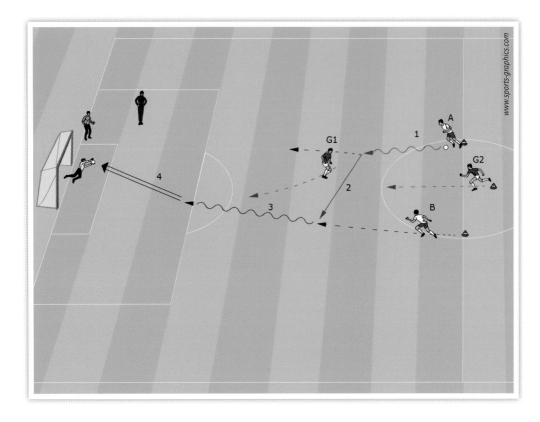

# 2 v 1 + 1

## Progression

Two offensive players try to outplay one defender (G1) at a high rate of speed. A pass past the opponent is followed by a fast dribble and shot at a large goal with goalkeeper. An additional player (G2) runs with A's first touch.

## Tips and suggestions

- The starting player estimates the distances and decides if he is fast enough to dribble toward the defender, and then outplay him with a through pass to his partner. If the distance to the opponent is too great, the starting player makes a through pass to his partner, who then challenges the defender.
- Player A must run along after the pass to B to provide another option for B. In doing so, he makes sure he doesn't go offside.
- G2's job is to support his teammate and put time pressure on the attackers. The goal is to turn the attacker's majority into an equal number.
- Depending on G1's defensive play, a double-pass from A to be B may also be a good solution.

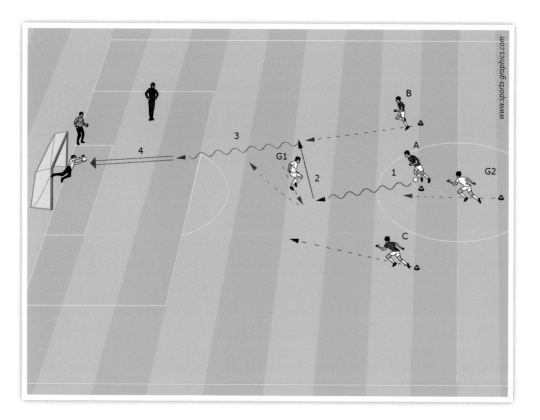

# 3 v 1 + 1

## Progression

Three offensive players carry out a quick attack against one defender (G1). Another defender (G2) starts approximately 2-3 yards behind the attackers. This creates a 3 v 2, plus goalkeeper.

## Tips and suggestions

Depending on the behavior of defender G1, A passes the ball to B or C.

Player A should do a fast dribble toward G1, so G2 is not able to intercept him. The pass should be made in such a way that a teammate is able control the ball at a high rate of speed.

The pass should be accurate and not too long, but also not played to the back.

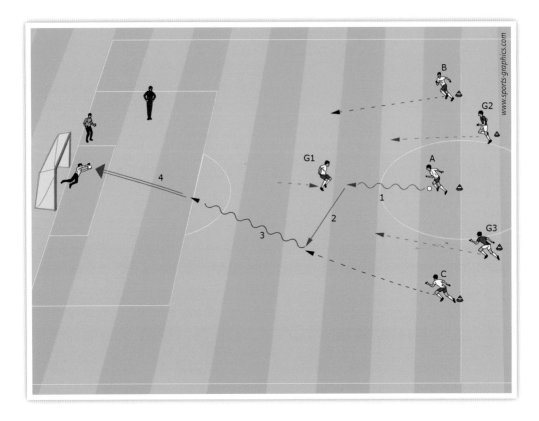

# 3 v 1 + 2

## Progression

Like the previous drill, but with an additional defender who puts time pressure on the attackers.

## Variation

• The defenders' starting positions should vary.

## Tips and suggestions

• Pay attention to offside.
• Dribble toward the defender (G1) and challenge him.
• Forwards C and B must cut to the inside in direction of the near post and not stay on the wings.

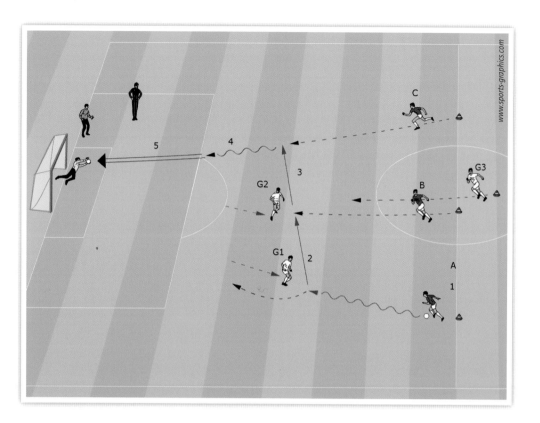

# 3 v 2 + 1

## Progression

In our example, A dribbles toward G1 at a high rate of speed and makes a through pass to B outside the goalkeeper's range. B plays a through pass to C as directly as possible and, after a brief fast dribble, finishes with a shot at the goal.

## Variation

- The center player runs and uses one of the two wing players. In doing so, he closely watches the behavior of the defenders (G1 and G2) and looks for an attack by G3.

## Tips and suggestions

- Player A dribbles toward G1 and challenges him.
- Fast and accurate passes from A to B, and finally to C.
- B creates a sufficient distance from G2 and plays the ball directly to C, or after a brief pass with C, before G3 has a chance to intervene.
- Depending on the defenders' behavior, the attackers should find their own creative solution.

## 2.4   From 1 v 2 to 8 v 8

### Preliminary remarks

While the counter attacks in the previous drills and games began with a stationary ball, the counter attack now starts with a game situation. This makes the practice realistic and competition-like. The object of the following game scenarios is to start a counter attack from a majority contest. In a square (5 x 5 yards up to 10 x 10 yards), the team with fewer players must dribble across a target line or pass to a teammate who is positioned behind the target line. The size of the square depends on the number and age or performance level of the players.

If the team with the minority loses possession of the ball, the other team immediately starts a counter attack.

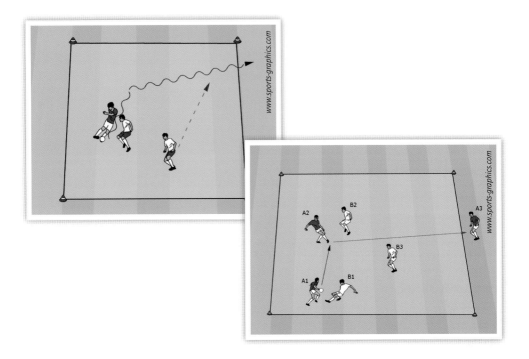

- The red player dribbles across the target line and gets a point.
- The red two-man team (A1, A2) manages to outplay the teammate (A3) behind the target line.

More and more players are added to the clearly arranged 1 v 2, and play becomes more and more complex. The players learn how to start a counter attack from a 1 v 1 situation. The running and passing lanes are not indicated but depend on the behavior of opponents and teammates.

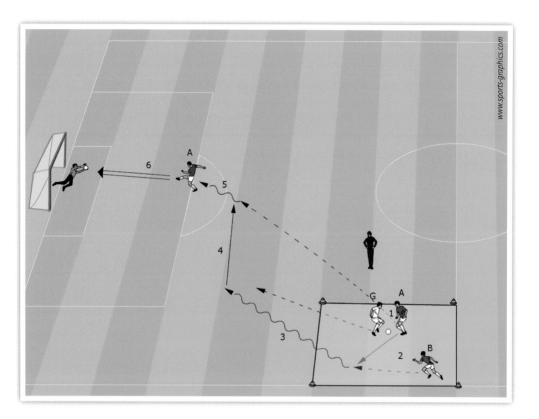

# 1 v 2

## Progression

One player (G) has the ball and tries to dribble to the target line against two others players in the square. When the two opposing players (A, B) steal the ball. they start a counter attack on the large goal. G chases the attackers, pressures them, and tries to win back the ball.

## Variation

- Start in the center or on the other side.

## Tips and suggestions

- There are several ways to continue after winning the ball. Each choice depends on the behavior of defensive players and teammates.
- A definite objective after gaining possession is to find the goal as quickly as possible and make a successful finish.
- Watch out for offside.

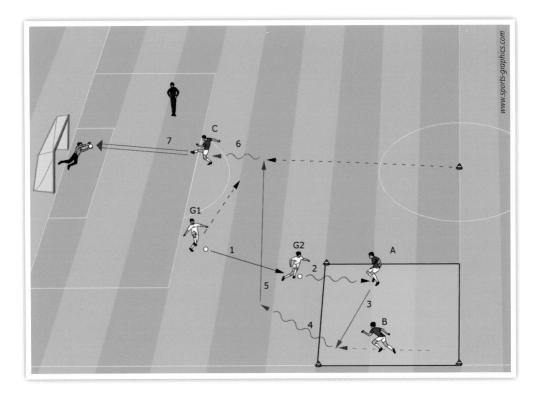

# 1 + 1 v 2 + 1

### Progression

From the penalty area, G1 plays to G2 who, just like in the previous contest, plays 1 v 2. G2 tries to dribble across the target line. A and B attack, and if they win the ball, they start a counter attack. After gaining possession, another player (C) runs from the centerline toward the goal to support A and B. G1 supports G2 in defending against the counter attack.

### Variation

• Start in the center or on the other side.

### Tips and suggestions

• It is important to have a time limit for the team launching the counter attack (5 - 6 seconds after winning the ball).
• The team launching the counter attack must be careful not to go offside.

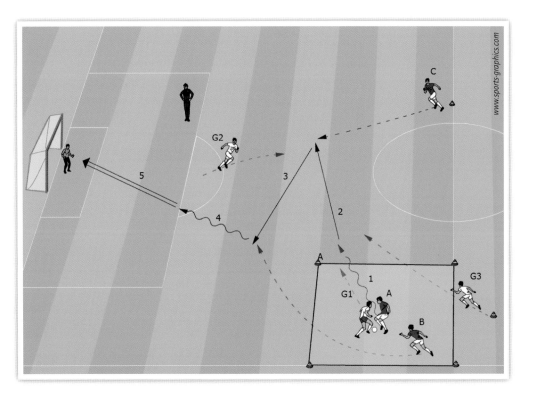

# 2 + 1 v 2 + 1

## Progression

G1 starts a 1 v 2 contest and tries to dribble across the target line or pass to G3. Players A and B try to prevent this and launch a counter attack when they gain possession of the ball. Once A wins the ball, B and C get involved in the counter attack.

At the same time, G3 gives chase and supports G1 and G2 in defending against the counter attack. In our example (see illustration), A wins the ball, dribbles toward the center of the field and is directly pressured by the pursuing G1. Player A makes a through pass to C, who is challenged by G2 and plays a through pass to B.

## Variation

• Start in the center or on the other side.

## Tips and suggestions

• C and B are careful not to go offside.
• The last pass to B must be accurately timed so he can control the ball at a run without delay to be able to quickly finish before G2 can reach him.

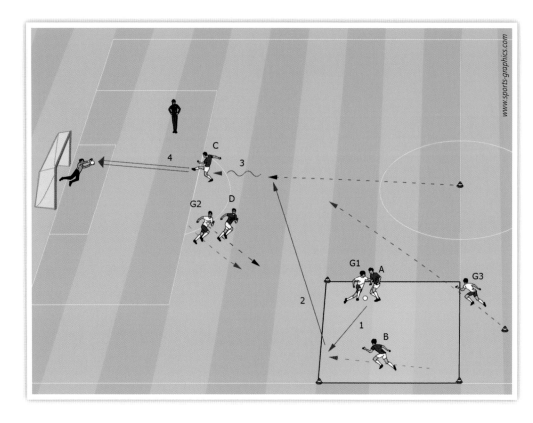

## 2 + 1 v 2 + 2

### Progression

In an 11 x 11-yard square, player G1 tries to dribble across a line or make a pass to teammate G3 behind the goal line. Players A and B try to prevent this. As soon as they win the ball, they start a counter attack with C and D at the large goal with the goalkeeper. G3 starts immediately after A or B wins the ball and helps G1 and G2 defend against the counter attack.

### Variation

- Start in the center or on the other side.

### Tips and suggestions

- Good cooperation between the offensive players is important to avoid delays and to quickly finish the counter attack.
- The offensive players must quickly register the movements of all teammates and defensive players, and skillfully and quickly utilize their majority.

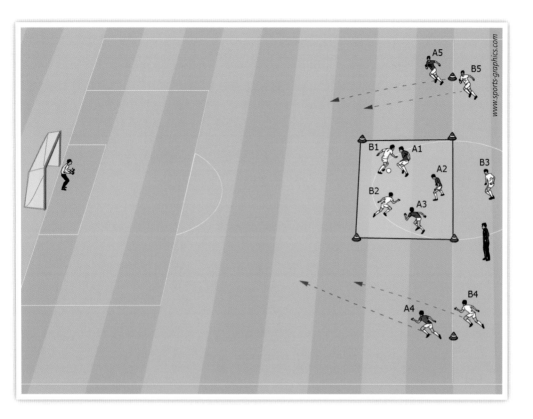

# 2 + 3 v 3 + 2

## Progression

Play is 2 v 3 at the centerline of a rectangle/square. The outnumbered team B tries to dribble across the target line or make a pass to their teammate (B3) behind the target line. Two additional defensive and offensive players are positioned near the sidelines. The counter attack begins when team A wins the ball.

## Tips and suggestions

- The outside forwards cut to the inside and avoid an offside.
- After winning the ball, the three midfield players cannot delay and must quickly play into the zone, or to A4 or A5.
- Watch out for offside.

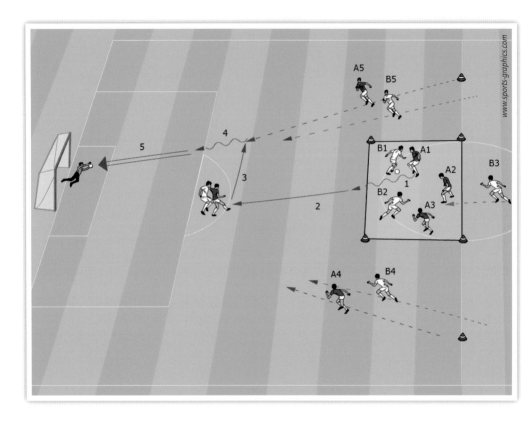

## 6 v 6 (2 v 3 + 3 v 2 + 1 v 1)

### Progression

Like the previous contest, but with an additional defender and forward near the penalty box.

### Tips and suggestions

- After winning the ball, it should be played into the zone as fast as possible. Ideally, A2 plays to the center forward who shields the ball and skillfully uses one of the offensive players who are moving up.

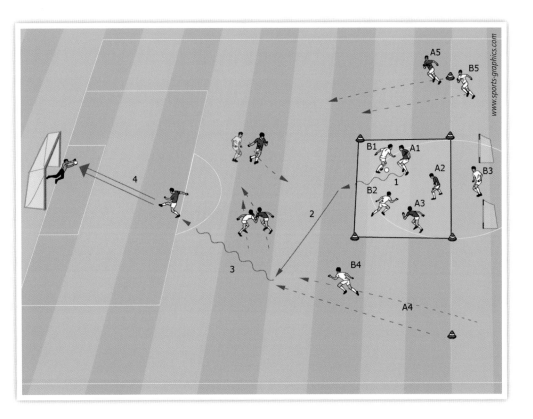

# 7 v 7 (2 v 3 + 3 v 2 + 2 v 2)

## Progression

Like the previous exercise, but with an additional defender and forward near the penalty box. The goal for B1 and B2 is to dribble across the target line or to score a goal from the rectangle/square in one of the two mini goals. The counter attack starts when team A wins the ball.

## Tips and suggestions

- This complex form of play requires that all players have a good overview of the game so they can be aware of any movements by teammates and opponents, and will be able to quickly make the right decisions.
- Direction and timing of passes, as well as coordinated running, become more important.
- The trainer sets a time limit (e.g., 8-12 seconds) so the counter attack does not turn into a possession attack, and the players look for a quick scoring opportunity.

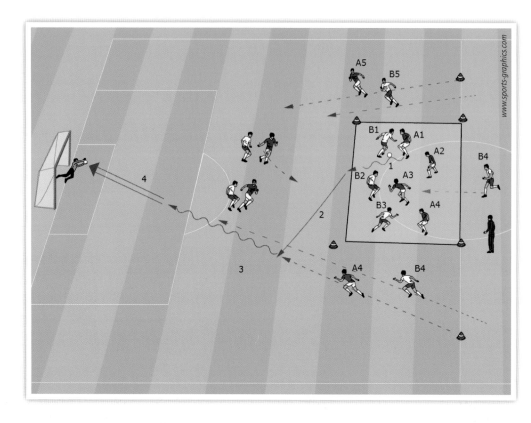

www.sports-graphics.com

# 8 v 8 (3 v 4 + 3 v 2 + 2 v 2)

## Progression

Like the previous exercise, but with the addition of a starting rectangle, another defender (B3), and another forward (A4). The goal of players B1, B2 and B3 is to pass to teammate B4 or to dribble across the target line so they can then score a point. The counter attack starts when team A wins the ball.

## Tips and suggestions

- All players make sure they choose the right moment for their actions (getting open, starting down field, passing).
- The trainer sets a time limit (e.g., 8-12 seconds) so the counter attack does not turn into a possession attack, and the players look for a quick scoring opportunity.

## 2.5    Competitions and drills

The following segment focuses on the counter attack with a finish after a 1 v 1, and small games played on four small goals with emphasis on counter attack play.

We will close with a 7 v 7 game of possession, in which the counter attack on the opposing goal begins after a certain number of touches or a signal from the trainer.

The players apply in smaller contests and drills what they have learned during the practices. Only when they are able to counter attack quickly and reliably under the pressure of competition has the training been successful.

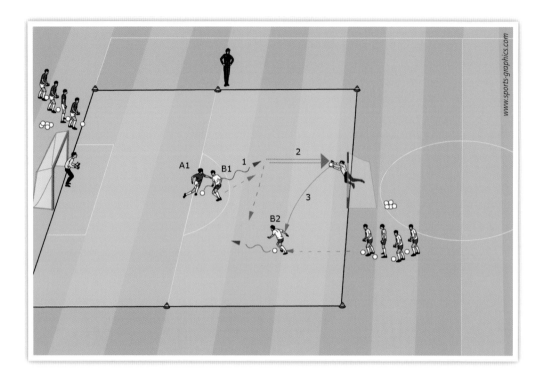

## 1 v 1 competition

### Progression

A 1 v 1 competition is played on a 40 x 40m field. The players from two teams wait behind their own goal line. In the center, two players compete for the first ball that the trainer kicks or throws into the center. Whoever wins the ball (here: A1) becomes the attacker and tries to score a goal in a 1 v 1 scenario (here: B1). If the ball goes into the goal or misses, A1 immediately becomes a defender against B2, who immediately starts the next counter attack with a shot at the goal. If the goalkeeper saves the ball, the game continues with a throw-out to B2, who starts a counter attack.

### Variations
- 2 v 2
- 3 v 3

### Tips and suggestions
- The various finishing positions will create many different counter attack situations.
- Allow for enough breaks – ensure a good balance between work phase and recovery.
- Excellent offensive and defensive 1 v 1-training.

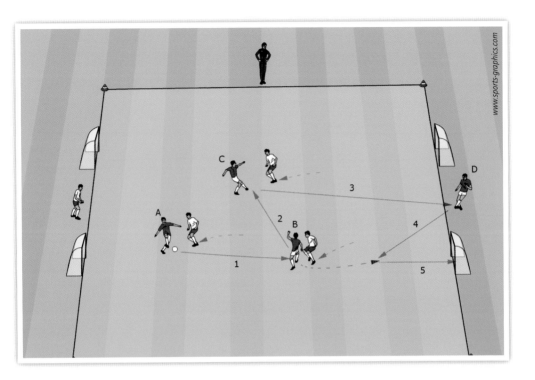

# 3+ 1 v 3 + 1

## Progression

3 v 3 play in a 21 x 21-yard square. Each team has an additional player behind the goal line between the two mini goals.

## Variation – 3 v 3 + 2 neutral players

- The outside players are neutral, and the direction of play changes when a goal is scored (counter attack against an unorganized defense). Back passes to neutral players are not allowed.

## Tips and suggestions

- Quick changeover after getting possession.
- Fast play down the field.
- Triangle formation after playing down the field.

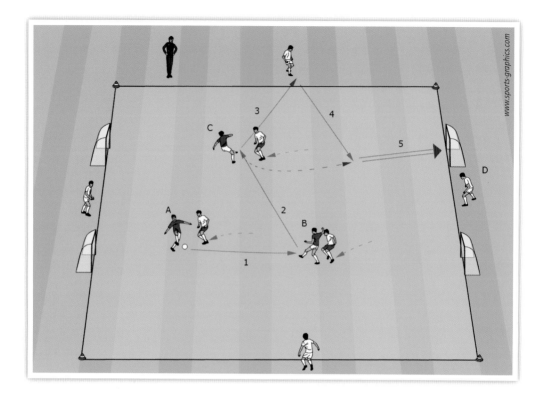

## 3 v 3 + 4 neutral receiving players

### Progression

Play is 3 v 3 on a 21 x 21-yard field. The four neutral players (two behind the goal, two at the sidelines) play with the team in possession of the ball. A back pass to the neutral player behind the goal is not allowed. After a goal is scored, the offensive team remains in possession and, as quickly as possible, launches an attack on the other side against the temporarily unorganized opponent.

### Variations

- 4 v 4 with four neutral players off the field (27 x 44 yards).
- In case of an odd number of players, a neutral player assists on the field.

### Tips and suggestions

- Quick changeover from defense to offense.
- Fast play down the field.
- Triangle formation.
- Double passes.
- Limited touches for neutral players (direct or two touches).

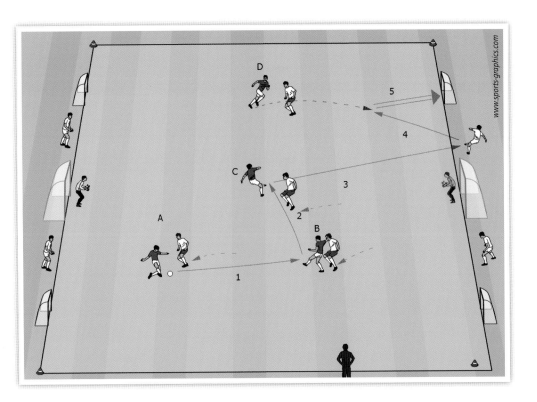

## Play with four mini and two large goals

### Progression

Play is 4 v 4 with four small and two large goals on a 33 x 44-yard field. Two neutral players are positioned behind each of the goal lines. A goal scored in a large goal is worth two points, in the small outer goals one point. Both teams change the direction of play after a goal is scored.

### Variations

- Two teammates behind the goals; direction of play does not change.
- Neutral players may join in play just once.
- Vary the number of touches on the field and behind the goals depending on the training objective and level of play.
- 5 v 5
- 6 v 6

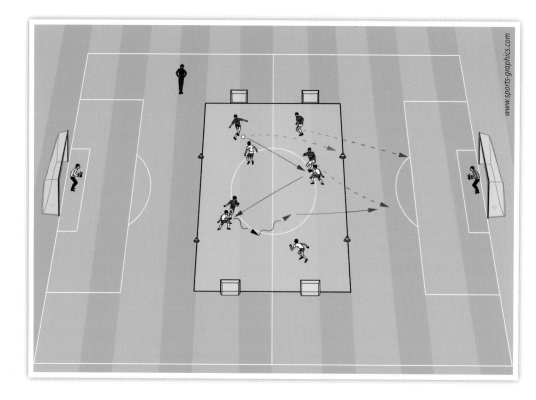

## 4 v 4 from the center

### Progression

Two teams play 4 v 4 on four small goals in the center of a 33 x 44-yard field. At the trainer's signal, the players switch over to a counter attack on a designated small goal. If the opposing team captures the ball, it launches a counter attack on the other side. Afterward, the game continues in the center.

### Variations

- 5 v 5 (field dimensions 33 x 54 yards).
- Free choice of goal (attack to the left and right of neutral goalkeeper).
- Goals are designated (e.g., A, B, or red, blue). The trainer calls out the letter or color, and the players must react accurately during the game situation (complex reaction drill).

### Tips and suggestions

- The players must start a counter attack on a large goal from a 4 v 4 (5 v 5) playing scenario. After a signal from the trainer, they should take advantage of the opponent's temporary disorganization to launch a very quick counter attack from the playing zone in direction of the goal.
- Training alertness and game overview.

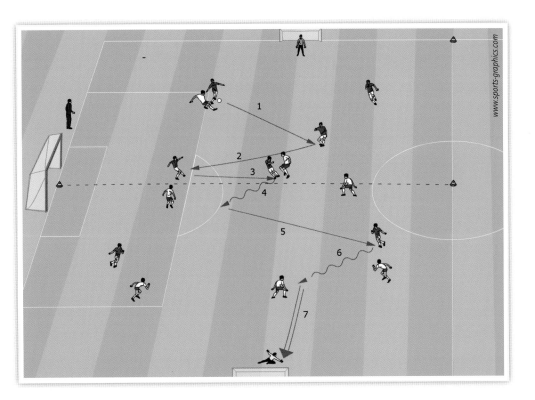

## 7 v 7 diagonally

### Progression

Two teams play 7 v 7 for possession on one half of the field. The attack on the goal beyond the centerline starts after a certain number of touches (e.g., six) or a signal from the trainer.

Example: After the sixth pass in field A, the counter attack on the goal in field B begins.

### Tips and suggestion

- The team in possession of the ball already braces for the counter attack before the sixth pass.
- The players carefully watch the positions of teammates and opponents to be able to quickly make the right decisions after the sixth pass.

# II  *Positional play*

## 3  Introduction

### 3.1  Positional play as prerequisite to the successful attack

The most important prerequisite to successful attacks is the ability of the entire team to keep the ball within their ranks under pressure. Ball possession does not guarantee winning, but it means setting the pace and rhythm of the game and, most importantly, it forces the opponent to do lots of running. The world's best teams distinguish themselves by nearly perfectly safeguarding and handling the ball in all game situations. They are masters at steadily building their game from the back under pressure. Most important to keeping possession of the ball is the play without the ball and mastering various and accurate passing techniques, even at the fastest speed. During training, small and big positional plays are particularly well suited for learning to keep possession of the ball. Alternating majority, equal, and inferior numbers is very important in the players' training. The field dimensions depend on the training objectives and the number of available players. A nearly perfectly positional play, like that of the Netherlands or FC Barcelona, must be systematically practiced from the very beginning.

### 3.2  Coaching points for positional play practice

- Immediately after winning and securing the ball, the field should be opened up and expanded by fanning out.
- Sides and center of field should be occupied.
- Players positioned at the sides of the field should be facing the field. (The players playing the gaps should also not stand with their backs to the field but open slightly diagonally to one side.)
- Getting permanently open near and away from the ball (depending on position of ball, opponent, and teammate, they continue to adjust their own position on the field).
- Coordinated position changes.
- Majority on the ball and triangle formation.
- Constantly play the gaps.

- Shifting play forces the opponent to do more running.
- Avoid unnecessary dribbling and risky passes.
- First-class passing play and mastery of all passing techniques.

The importance of the so-called first touch when controlling the ball in connection with the passing game must be emphasized again and again. When Ronaldinho controls the ball, he always prepares subsequent action with the first touch so he can immediately play a planned pass, center the ball, or take a direct shot at the goal.

One important prerequisite for this is that the player receiving the pass recognizes what his options are for continued play and which of these might be the best option, before the ball reaches him. "Stop – look – play" has been obsolete and outdated for decades.

## 3.3    Play without the ball

Soccer is largely a game without the ball. During a game, each player has an average possession of only 1.5-2 minutes. The biggest part of the game consists of various running movements, such as walking, jogging, sprinting, etc. The movements of players without the ball must be coordinated and must open up as many good passing options as possible.

These coordinated movements must make the opponent's defensive work more difficult and depend on the particular game situation. The man on the ball should always have options for short and long passes. Which option he chooses depends on his tactical assessment of the game situation. Getting open means either breaking away from his opponent so he cannot interfere with his receiving the ball, or the player getting open gets himself in a position that opens a big passing angle for the player in possession.

As spatial, opposing, and time pressures continue to grow, the running body feint becomes increasingly more important when trying to get open. First, an intention is faked with a contrary running motion. The player getting open utilizes his mental head start, which he turns into a moving head start with his subsequent run in the intended direction after his body feint. A player gets open by changing his running direction or running speed.

## 3.4    Additional tips for getting open

- Get out of the opponent's marking zone (shadow) into open areas to play and function.
- Do not get open without an eye on the ball and on your teammates.

## 3.5     The importance of passing

The pass is the most common action in a game. According to Jens Bangsbo and Birger Peitersen, up to 800 passes are played in the course of a game. Doucet claims, "The pass is the soul of the soccer game!" The pass is the building stone that makes collective play possible.

In many sports, the simplest movement or technical execution is also the most difficult because players (and also many trainers) often underestimate these movements and therefore do not practice them enough. Every player can make some kind of pass and the ball most often will reach the teammate but passing play must nevertheless be a regular part of training. Every tennis player spends the bulk of his practice time hitting simple forehand strokes, and anyone who has observed a professional club practice will know that even the stars do many passing drills.

A good passing game is characterized by precision, the right speed, and accurate timing.

## 3.6     Practicing game-appropriate and two-footed passing

However, too often the passing game is still practiced in the so-called passing alley. Two players face each other and pass the ball back and forth.

This set-up may be practical for recognizing and correcting technical deficiencies, but it is neither motivating nor realistic. This is true especially when considering the various types of passes that must be used for respective tactical backgrounds (position of ball, teammate, opponents, or the respective distances to each other).

We are familiar with the chip pass, square pass, back or diagonal pass, the short and long pass, the low pass, medium pass, and high pass, the double pass, as well as the pass under time and counter pressure. Most of these passes must not only be played hard but must also be played with precision to facilitate the desired continuation of play.

In terms of game-appropriate training, we should also meet these requirements as much as possible with passing drills. Therefore, most drills should be diversified with other emphases (signaling availability, getting open, triangle formation, making and using space, moving up, changing position, etc.).

This also includes organizing the assignment of tasks in such a way that the players must pass with both feet, as well as variations with limited touches or guidelines that require, for instance, that the ball must be received and turned in a different direction with the first touch and must be played again with the second touch.

## 3.7　The ten most important coaching points for passing practice

1. Passing accuracy
2. Hardness of pass based on situation
3. Passes should be as low as possible (they reach their target quicker and are easier to control)
4. Optimal timing of pass
5. Use running feints
6. Coordinated movement of players
7. Using both feet
8. Generally playing the ball to the foot away from the opponent
9. Depth before width (also in passing drills)
10. Coaching (good verbal and nonverbal communication). Among other things, this includes eye contact between passing player and receiving player.

## 3.8　Corrections

- For flat passes ball contact should be central, for high balls contact from below.
- To pass, use momentum rather than strength.
- Passing with the inside foot is safest and most accurate, but also easiest to read. Passing with the outside foot is less obvious and smoother, but due to the much smaller contact area, it is technically clearly more difficult.
- The player getting open determines the timing, direction, and type of pass.

# 4 Preparatory drills for positional play

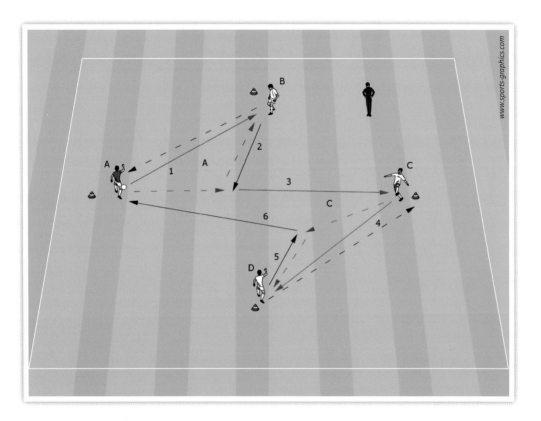

www.sports-graphics.com

## 4.1 Diamond – basic drill

### Progression

This is the basic form of the diamond drill. Passing and receiving players constantly change positions. Player A plays to B (1) and runs to the center of the diamond. B makes a through pass to A (2) and runs to position A. Player A makes a direct pass to C (3) and takes the place of B. C makes a direct pass to D and runs to the center of the diamond. D makes a through pass to C and runs to position C. C passes directly to A and takes the place of D.

### Variations

- Pay attention to accuracy of passes and using both feet.
- Low passes.
- Use running feints.

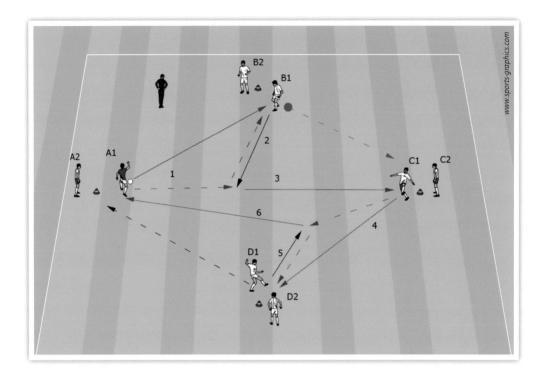

## 4.2   Diamond – variation 1

### Progression

This is a variation of the passing game in the diamond. The receiving player doesn't change positions with the passing player but runs in playing direction to the next passing player. A1 plays to B1 (1) and runs to the center of the diamond. B1 makes a through pass to A1 (2) and runs to position C. A1 makes a direct pass to C1 (3) and takes the place of B1. C1 makes a direct pass to D1 and runs to the center of the diamond. D1 makes a through pass to C1 and runs to position A. C1 makes a direct pass to A2 and takes the place of D1.

### Variation

- Play from the right side.

### Tips and suggestions

- Pay attention to accuracy of passes and using both feet.
- Low passes.
- Use running feints.

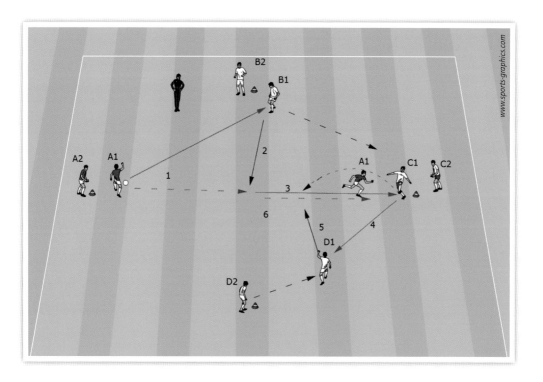

## 4.3    Diamond – variation with opposing player

### Progression

This is the target exercise in the diamond. After the initial give and go, the passing player (here A1) attacks the next passing player (here C1) after his high pass. Next comes a double pass. A1 plays to B1 (1) and runs to the center of the diamond. B1 makes a through pass to A1 (2) and runs to position C. A1 makes a direct pass to C1 (3) and takes the place of B1. C1 makes a direct pass to D1 and runs to the center of the diamond. D1 makes a through pass to C1 and runs to position A. C1 makes a direct pass to A2 and takes the place of D1.

### Variations

- Play from the right side.
- The passing player fakes a double pass and dribbles past the attacker.

### Tips and suggestions

- The passing player only makes a direct pass when the attacking player has gotten close enough. Otherwise, he plays the double pass after a brief possession of the ball.
- Use running feints.

# 5   Games for positional play

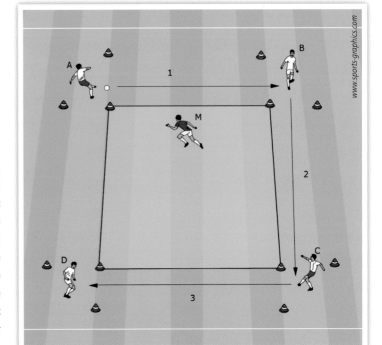

## 4 v 1 in a corridor

### Progression

Four players pass the ball in a corridor. During the first stage, they can have two touches; during the second stage, they can have one touch. Another player, who is also allowed to enter the corridor, tries to intercept the ball from the center with a cunning run.

### Tips and suggestions

- The size of the field and the width of the corridor depend on the players' skill level. The smaller the field and the narrower the corridor, the more difficult the job for the wing players.
- Depending on the type of defense played, the defender plays the most reliable pass.
- The wing players ideally pass clockwise with the right foot and counter-clockwise with the left foot.
- The wing players should assume an open posture.

### Objectives

- Reliable passing (90°).
- Recognize best passing options.

### Competitions

- Complete a specific number of passes.

### Variation: get a free touch after 10 passes.

- Which defender wins the ball the most during a predetermined amount of time?

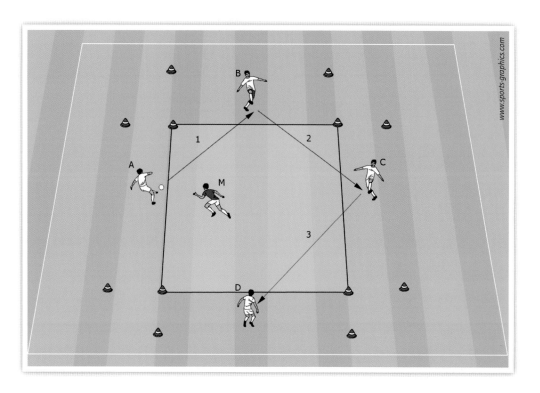

www.sports-graphics.com

## 4 v 1 in a diamond

### Progression

Four players pass each other the ball through a square with two touches (beginners) or directly (more advanced). The ball must be played through the square. The wing players are not allowed to leave their zone. The center player can play anywhere.

### Tips and suggestions
- Open posture.
- Be aware of all options.
- Get out of the cover shadow.

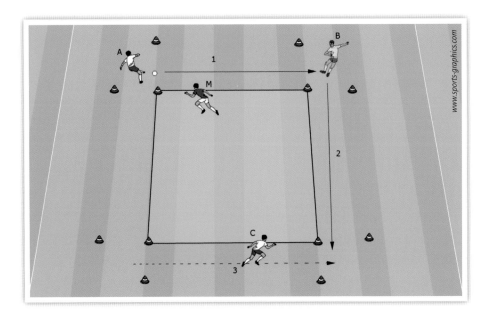

# 3 v 1 in a corridor

## Progression

Three players pass each other the ball in a corridor. One corner of the square is always open. The receiving player starts for that corner. The man on the ball must always have two passing options. One player tries to intercept the ball from the center with a clever run.

## Tips and suggestions
- The size of the field and the width of the corridor depend on the players' skill level. The smaller the field and the narrower the corridor, the more difficult the job for the wing players.
- The passing player is definitely free and does not have to try to get open.

## Objectives
- Learn how to get open, run into open space.
- Reliable passing game.
- Get out of the cover shadow.
- Smart defensive play.

## Competitions
- Complete a specific number of passes.

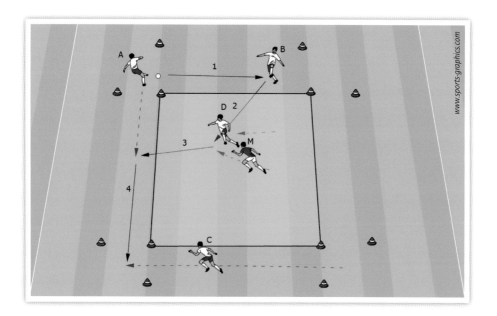

# 3 + 1 v 1 in a corridor

## Progression

Three players pass each other the ball, through a corridor to a wing player or to the teammate in the center. One defender in the center tries to win the ball with a cunning run.

## Tips and suggestions

- The size of the field depends on the players' skill level. The smaller the field, the more difficult the job for the wing players.

## Objectives

- Getting open.
- Reliable passing game.
- Recognize best passing options.
- Get out of the cover shadow.
- Smart defensive play.

## Competitions

- Complete a specific number of passes.

## Variation

- Two touches or direct play (advanced players).

## 3 v 1 in a square

### Progression

Three players freely pass each other the ball in a square. One opposing player tries to get his foot on the ball (trap it). The side lengths of the square (6-11 yards) depend on the players' skill level.

### Variations

- Open play
- Two touches
- 2-3 mandatory touches
- Direct play

### Tips and suggestions

- Main principle: The passing player always takes the short path out of the cover shadow.
- Also good as a handball game: practice getting open.

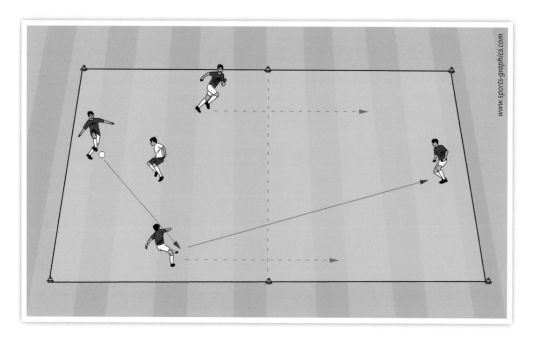

www.sports-graphics.com

# 3 v 1 + 1 with shifting play

### Progression

Players in the first square play 3 v 1. In the second square, one player waits for the pass from a wing player. Two players immediately move up and play 3 v 1 on the second field with the fourth player. The defender runs onto the second field and attacks.

### Variations

- There is a corridor between the two squares.
- Two touches by the wing players.
- Direct play.

### Training objectives

- Deep forward passes.
- Support the player going down the field (move up).
- Triangle formation.
- Shift play.

### Tips and suggestions

- The fourth player should be open as far back as possible and always ready.
- Add breaks, high intensity.

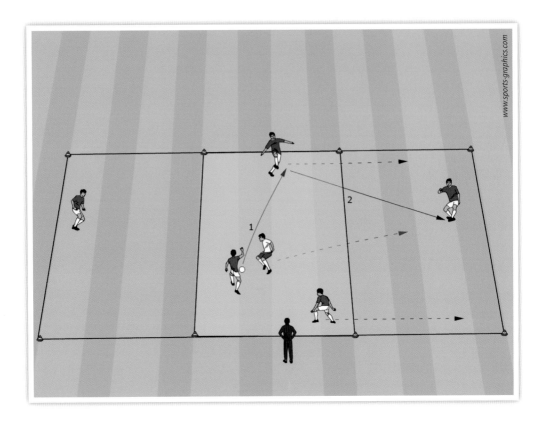

## 3 + 2 v 1

### Progression

Play is 3 v 1 in the center square. Two teammates are positioned in the outside squares. After a shift in play, two players immediately move up to one of the other two fields for a new 3 v 1. The defender gives chase and continues to attack. Whoever makes a mistake becomes the defender.

### Training objectives

- Deep forward passes.
- Shift play and move up.
- Triangle formation.

### Variations

- There is a corridor between the two squares.
- Two touches.
- Direct play.

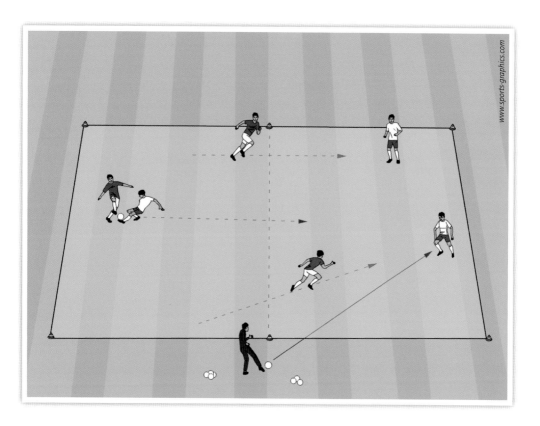

www.sports-graphics.com

# 3 v 1 as a team competition

## Progression

Three red players play against one blue player on one field. Two other blue players wait on the field on the right. After a touch or a turnover, the coach plays the ball to one of the blue players on the right field. The blue defender runs onto the right field and supports his teammates. A red player becomes the defender and attacks the three blue players on the right field.

## Variation

• A few balls are placed at the goal line so the game can be played without passes from the trainer.

## Training objectives

• Deep forward passes.
• Shift play and move up.
• Triangle formation.

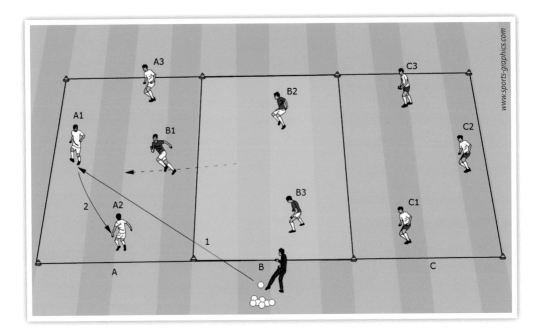

## 3 v 1 with three colors

### Progression

To start, three teams of three are each positioned in an 8 x 8-yard square (A, B, C). The trainer plays a ball onto the left starting field A (1). One player from the group in the center starts from the right half of the center field B and attacks the white players. After 10 passes and a shift in play to field C, the white team gets one point. The players in the center are not allowed to intercept the pass to shift play. When a mistake is made (touch), tasks change. The red players move onto the left field and white changes to the center. The trainer immediately plays a ball onto the right field and a white player attacks.

Who can make the most shifts in play?

### Variations

*   4 v 2
*   5 v 3

### Tips and suggestions

*   Shift in play.
*   Short passes.

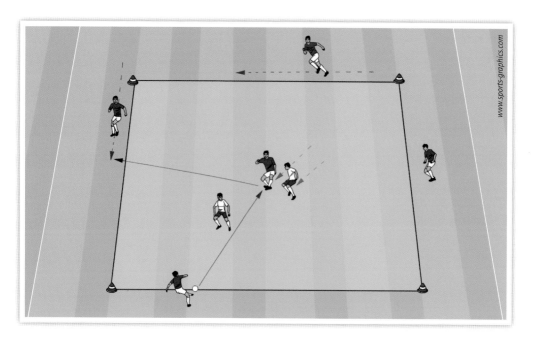

# 4 + 1 v 2

## Progression

Four players pass a ball form their zone through the square to a wing player or to the teammate in the center. Two defenders in the center together try to win the ball. The player in the center only moves within the inner square.

## Variation

- Two touches or direct play.

## Tips and suggestions

- The size of the field depends on the players' skill level. The smaller the field, the more difficult the job for the wing players.
- The player in the center always plays the gap and facilitates triangles.

## Objectives

- Triangle formation.
- Reliable passing.
- Getting open.
- Recognize the best passing options.
- Get out of the cover shadow.

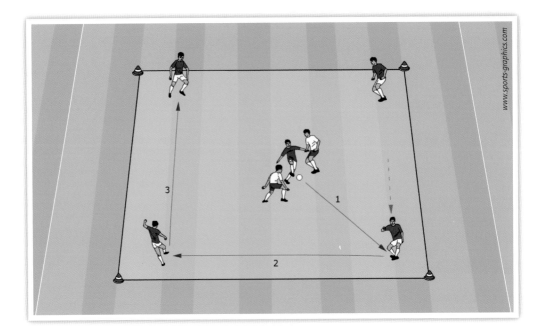

## 5 v 2

### Progression

Five players play against two defenders.

### Variations

- Number of touches according to players' skill level.
- Two mandatory touches.

### Tips and suggestions

- Create many passing options for the man on the ball.
- Triangle formation.
- Man the gaps.
- Open posture.

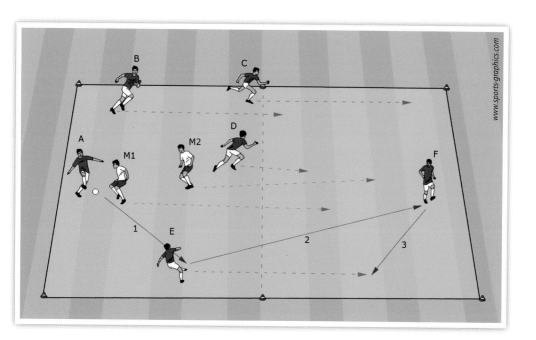

# 5 + 1 v 2 with shifting play

## Progression

On the left field, players play 5 v 2 without touch limits. After a shift in play to player F, four offensive players and the two defenders move up to the other field for another 5 v 2. One player stays on the left field for the next shift in play. Whoever makes a mistake becomes the defender, and the player who has been in the center the longest becomes the wing player.

## Variations

- Two touches
- Direct play
- 5 v 2 with three colors (analogous to 3 v 1)
- 5 v 2 as a team competition (analogous to 3 v 1)

## Tips and suggestions

- Shift play and move up.
- The player waiting on the other field should constantly adjust his position.
- Create many passing options for the man on the ball.
- Triangle formation.
- Man the gaps.
- Open posture.

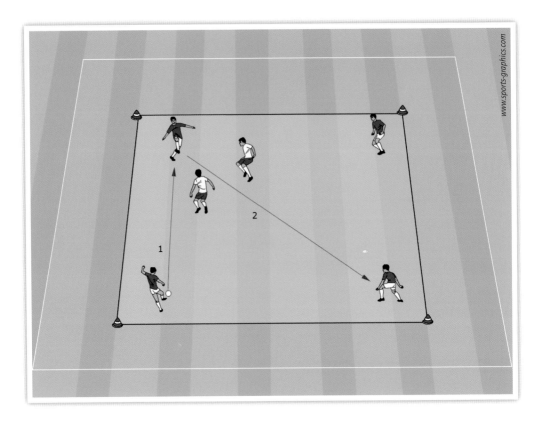

# 4 v 2

## Progression

Four wing players pass each other the ball in a square (11 x 11 yards) and are attacked by two defenders. Whoever makes a mistake becomes the defender, and the player who is in the center longest becomes the wing player.

## Variations

- Two touches
- Direct play (pro version)

## Tips and suggestions

- Teammates create as many passing stations as possible for the man on the ball (play the gaps and sides).
- Get out of the cover shadow.
- Run into open space.

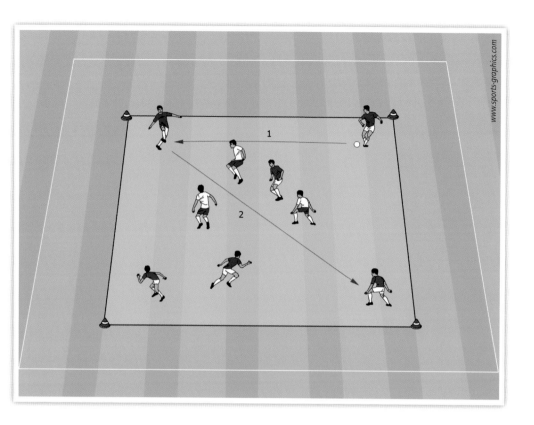

www.sports-graphics.com

# 6 v 3

## Progression

Play is 6 v 3. Whoever makes a mistake becomes the defender, and the player who is in the center longest becomes the wing player.

## Variations

- Two touches
- Direct play (pro version)

## Tips and suggestions

- Optimal coverage of the field – ideally four players on the wings at the sidelines and two players in the center.
- Man the gaps.
- Wing and midfield players maintain open posture.
- Triangle formation.

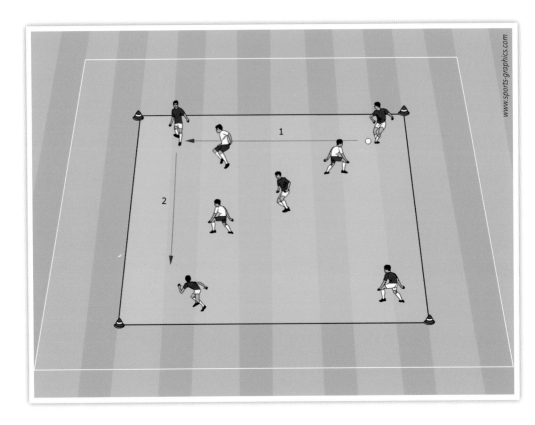

## 5 v 3

### Progression

Play is 5 v 3. Whoever makes a mistake becomes the defender, and the player who is in the center longest becomes the wing player.

### Variation

• Two touches

### Tips and suggestions

• Optimal coverage of the field – ideally four players on the wings at the lines and one player in the center.
• Man the gaps.
• Wing and midfield players maintain open posture.
• Center player facilitates triangle formation.

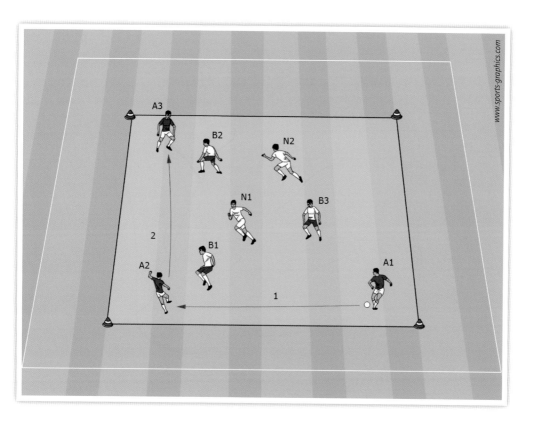

# 3 v 3 + 2 neutral players on the field

## Progression

Play is 3 v 3, in a square (21 x 21 yards – depending on skill level), with two neutral players. The neutral players always play with the team in possession of the ball and are changed after a predetermined amount of time. After a certain number of passes, the team in possession of the ball gets a point.

## Variation

- Touches according to players' skill level (open play, three touches, two touches, direct).

## Tips and suggestions

- Quick changeover from offense to defense and vice versa.
- Optimal coverage of the field.
- Man the gaps.
- Wing and midfield players maintain open posture.
- Center player facilitates triangle formation.

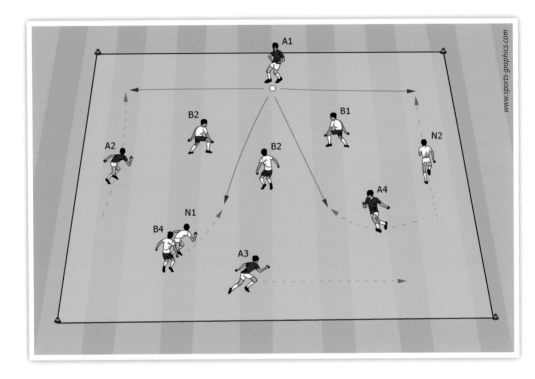

## 4 v 4 + 2 neutral players on the field

### Progression

Play is 4 v 4, in a rectangle (32 x 21 yards), with two neutral players. After a certain number of passes, the team in possession of the ball gets a point.

Playing time is 5 x 3 minutes. Each player takes one turn as a neutral player.

### Tips and suggestions

- Good coverage of the field in depth and width.
- Man center and gaps.
- Open posture.

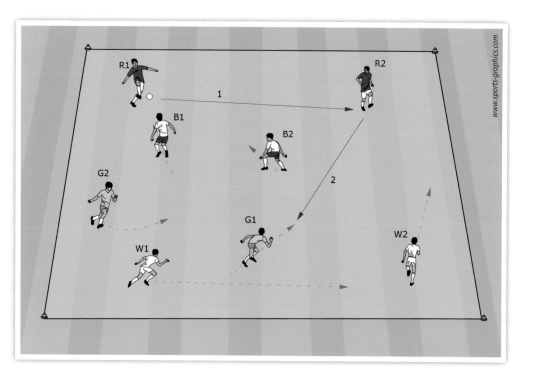

# 6 v 2 – four color play

## Progression
Six wing players (three pairs: red, gray, white) play against the blue players. When a mistake is made, the "mistake pair" moves to the center.

## Variations
- The pair playing defense must have two touches (one player with two touches or a pass to the partner) before they can leave the center.
- Opportunity to win back the ball – pressing.
- Cannot pass to a player of the same color (that would make it 5 v 2).
- 9 v 3 with four colors.
- 12 v 4 with four colors.

## Tips and suggestions
- Improve awareness and action speed.
- Good coverage of the field in depth and width.
- Man center and gaps.
- Open posture.

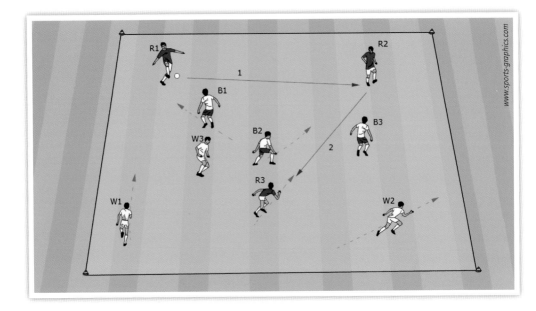

## 6 v 3 – three color play

### Progression

Six wing players (two groups of three: red and white) play in a rectangle (21 x 32 yards) against three blue players in the center. If a mistake is made, the "mistake threesome" moves to the center. The first ball after gaining possession is free.

### Variations

- Play continues immediately after gaining possession of the ball (immediate changeover).
- Defense must have two touches (two touches or one pass to a partner) before they can leave the center.
- Opportunity to win back the ball – pressing.

### Pro version

- Can only pass to the other color.
- 6 v 3 – open play with own color – one touch with other color.

### Tips and suggestions

- Improve awareness and action speed.
- Good coverage of the field in depth and width.
- Man center and gaps.
- Open posture.
- Guard the ball.

# 8 v 4 – three color play

## Progression

Eight wing players (two groups of four: red and white) play in a rectangle (32 x 42 yards) against four blue players in the center. If a mistake is made, the "mistake foursome" moves to the center. The first ball after gaining possession is free.

## Variations
- Play continues immediately after gaining possession of the ball (immediate changeover).
- Defense must have two touches (two touches or one pass to a partner) before they can leave the center.
- Opportunity to win back the ball – pressing.

## Pro version
- Passing only to the other color is allowed.
- 8 v 4 – open play with own color – one touch with other color.

## Tips and suggestions
- Improve awareness and action speed.
- Good coverage of the field in depth and width (two players on the two long sides and one player on the two short sides of the rectangle, and two players in the center).
- Man gaps.

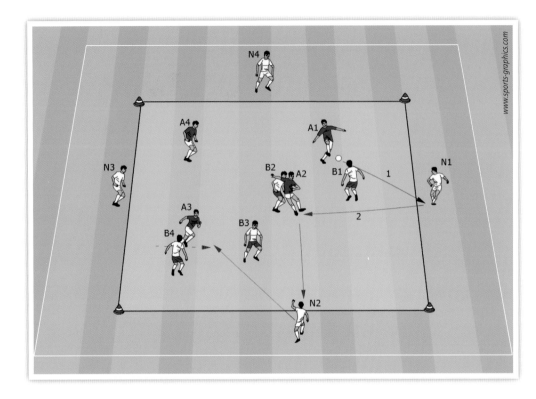

## 4 v 4 + 4 outlying neutral players

### Progression

Play is 4 v 4 in a square (32 v 32 yards). Outside the square are four neutral players who play with the team in possession of the ball. The neutral players cannot play together. After a predetermined amount of time (3-4 minutes), one of the inside teams switches to the outside and becomes neutral.

### Variations

- Neutral players can only play to each other once.
- Limited touches, especially for outside players.

### Tips and suggestions

- Active recovery is particularly important for the team with two consecutive turns in the center.
- Triangle formation, especially after a pass to an outside player.
- Immediate changeover after gaining possession.

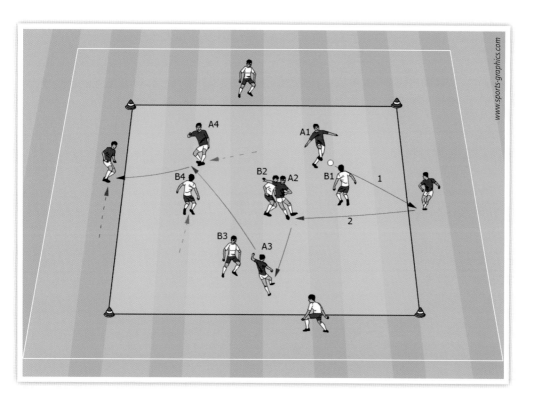

# 4 + 2 v 4 + 2 in a square

## Progression

Play is 4 v 4 in the center square. Each team has two outside players. The four inside players together with their two outside players try to keep possession of the ball.

## Variation

- One position change from outside to inside within one's own team is allowed. The outside player receiving the pass switches to the inside of the square after his pass or dribbles the ball to the inside. An inside player takes over his position.

## Scoring

- 10 passes = one point

## Tips and suggestions

- Improve awareness and action speed.
- Change positions.
- Triangle formation.

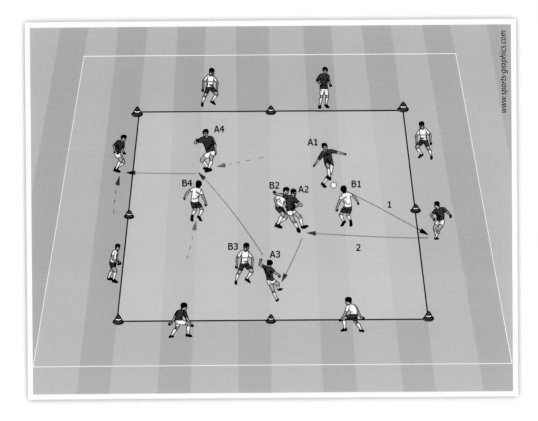

## 4 + 4 v 4 + 4 in a square

Progression

Like the previous positional drill, but now the sidelines of the square are divided into two sections. The red and blue players take turns there. The inside players guard the ball together with their four outside players.

Variations
- 5 + 4 v 5 + 4
- 3 + 4 v 3 + 4
- Two touches for inside players – outside players direct.
- The outside players can play to each other once.
- Outside and inside players change positions.
- Play with a third player (outside player cannot pass back to passing player).

Tips and suggestions
- After a pass to an outside player, the inside players form a triangle (triangle formation).
- Improve awareness and action speed.

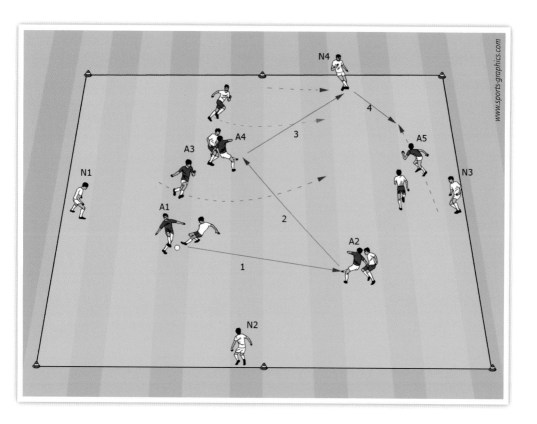

## 5 v 5 + 4 neutral players at the sidelines

### Progression

Play is 5 v 5 in a rectangle (65 x 43 yards). The team in possession of the ball plays together with the neutral players positioned at the four sidelines on the inside of the field.

### Variation

- Limited touches, especially for neutral players.

### Tips and suggestions

- Use goalkeepers as neutral players.
- Shift play via short passes and long balls and then move up.
- Create a majority near the ball.

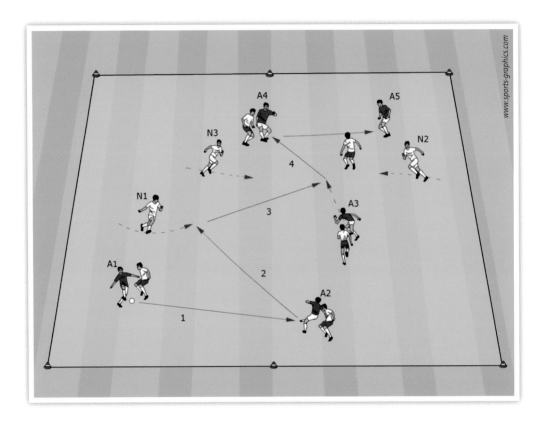

# 5 v 5 + 3 neutral players in a rectangle

## Progression

5 v 5 competition with three neutral players in a rectangle (65 x 43 yards). The attackers thus have an 8 v 5 advantage.

## Variation

•   Limited touches, especially for neutral players.

## Tips and suggestions

•   Shift in play.
•   Create a majority near the ball.
•   Quick changeover from defense to offense and vice versa.

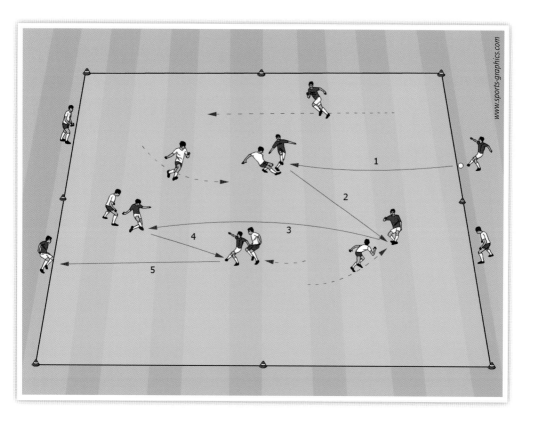

# 5 + 2 v 5 + 2

## Progression

Play is 5 v 5 on a field (43 x 32 yards). One teammate and one opposing player are positioned on the outside at each end of the field. The team in possession of the ball guards the ball and gets one point for 10 passes. It gets three points for a combination play by outside player to outside player (2-4 passes).

## Variation

- Change of position by inside and outside players is allowed.

## Tips and suggestions

- Shift in play.
- Quick play down the field.
- Guard the ball.

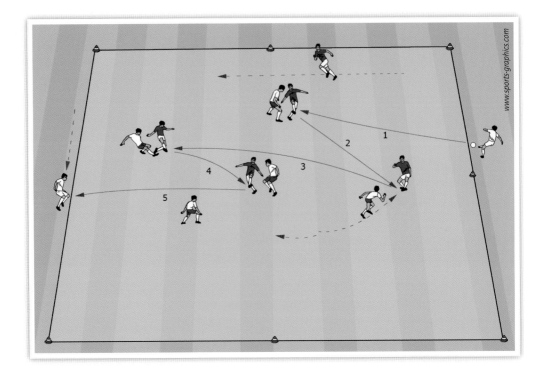

## 5 v 5 + 2 neutral players in the target zone

### Progression

Play is 5 v 5 on a field (43 x 32 yards). Two neutral players are positioned at the ends of the field. The team in possession of the ball gets one point for 10 passes without a touch by the opponent. If a team manages to make a combination play from one neutral outside player to the other (2-4 passes), it gets three points.

### Variations

- 2 v 2
- 3 v 3
- 4 v 4
- 6 v 6
- 7 v 7

### Tips and suggestions

- Shift in play.
- Quick play down the field.
- Guard the ball.
- The size of the field depends on the number and skill level of the players.

## From 8 v 2 to 8 v 8

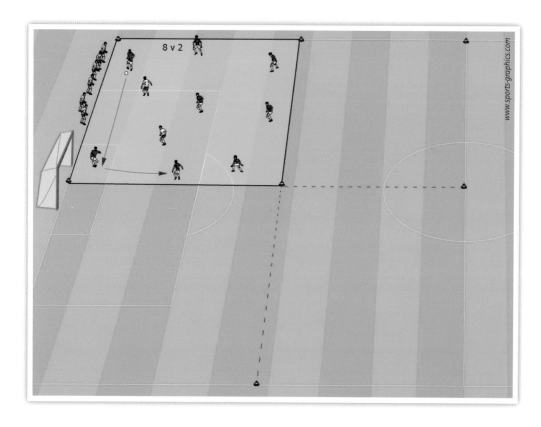

## Phase 1: 8 v 2 on a ⅛-size field

### Progression

The red team starts with an 8 v 2 and tries to keep possession of the ball as long as possible on ⅛ of the field. After the turnover, the red team's possession time is clocked. Then the tasks change. If the two blue players are not able to win the ball within 60 seconds, play changes from 8 v 2 to 8 v 4 on a ¼-size field.

### Variations

- The defenders must first play a pass to each other to gain possession of the ball.
- The attackers get two touches or must play direct.

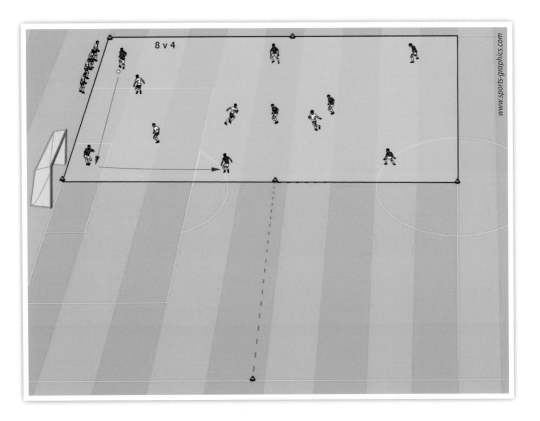

8 v 4

## Phase 2: 8 v 4 on a ¼-size field

Progression

During phase 2, play is 8 v 4. If the four defenders are unable to win the ball within 30 (60) seconds, phase 3 begins.

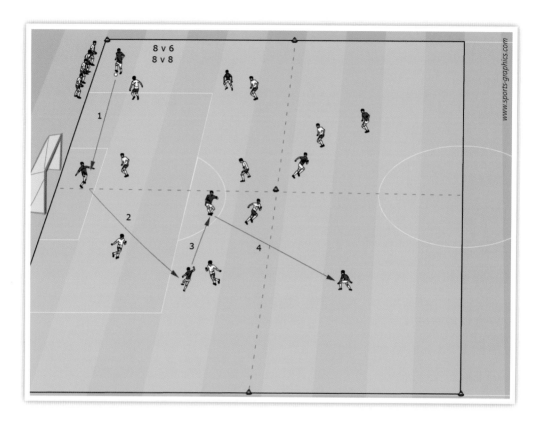

## Phase 3: 8 v 6 and 8 v 8 on ½ of the field

Progression

During phase 3, six defenders play against eight offensive players. If the six defenders are unable to win the ball within 30 (60) seconds, the attackers reach phase 4.

## Phase 4: 8 v 8 on one half of the field

During the final phase play is 8 v 8. How long can the offensive players keep possession of the ball? When the defenders win the ball, the trainer stops the clock. The team with the longest possession time wins the game.

Tips and suggestions
- Safeguard possession of the ball on different size fields and against a varying number of opponents.
- Number players consecutively.
- Use of a stopwatch is recommended.

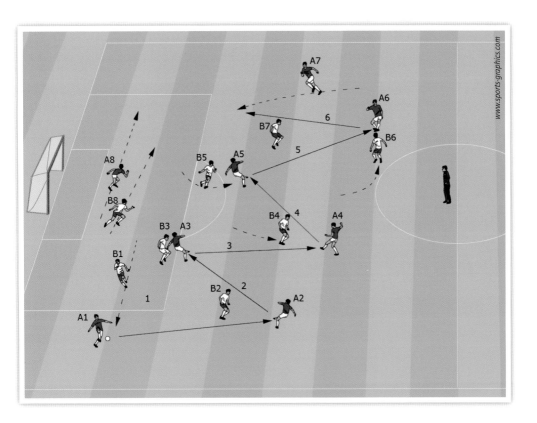

# 8 v 8 for possession

### Progression
Play is 8 v 8, for possession on ½ of a field. Eight consecutive passes are worth one point.

### Variation
- Who stays in possession for a certain amount of time (e.g., 30 seconds)?

### Tips and suggestions
- Safeguard possession.
- Get open.
- Use the entire field.
- A majority near the ball.
- Create as many passing options as possible for the man on the ball.

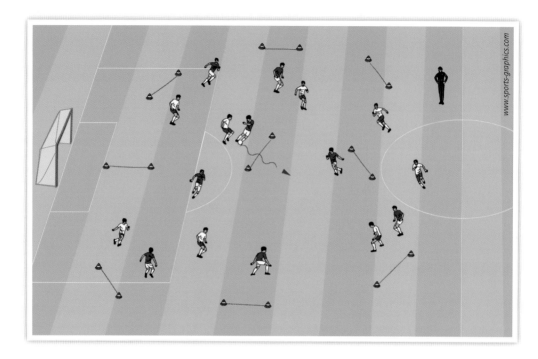

## 8 v 8 with nine cone goals

### Progression

Two teams play 8 v 8 with nine cone goals (open goals) on ½ of the field. A goal is valid when a player dribbles across the goal line.

### Additional scoring options

- Pass to a teammate through one goal with subsequent steady ball control.
- Pass through a goal and direct pass to a third player, who must demonstrate steady ball control.
- Combination of all three variations with varying scores (dribbling – one point, pass – two points, play with a third player – three points).

### Variation

- 7 v 7 with eight goals (always one goal more than players on a team).

### Tips and suggestions

- Good awareness and action speed.
- Safeguard possession.
- Quickly shift play to find an open goal.
- Create a majority.

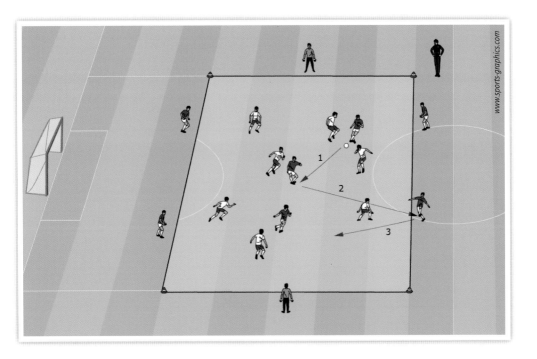

# 9 v 7 ("open and close")

## Progression

Play is 3 v 7 in a rectangle (43 x 32 yards). The three inside players safeguard possession of the ball with the support of four teammates on the long sides and two neutral players on the short sides. The three inside players have unlimited touches, all outside players have two touches or play direct. The two outside players on the long sides cannot play together. Outside players are allowed to pass to each other across the corners. If the seven blue players win the ball, four blue players must leave the field and move to the four outside positions, while three players remain on the field. The four red outside players run onto the field and support their three teammates to try and win back the ball.

## Tips and suggestions

- After gaining possession, it is important to safeguard the ball and to quickly man the outside positions on the long sides. After gaining possession, it is advisable to make the first pass to one of the neutral outside players.
- After losing the ball, the objective is to immediately put collective pressure on the three inside players.
- Apply the shortest path principle when leaving the field.
- Practice your awareness.
- Players coach each other.

# Setting training goals with a number of permitted touches

In games with a majority and neutral players, the trainer has a number of options for changing training emphasis by changing the permitted number of touches.

| Player | Neutral Player |
|---|---|
| Open | Open |
| Open | Two touches |
| Open | One touch |
| Three touches | Two touches |
| Two touches | One touch |
| One touch | Open |
| One touch | Open |
| One touch | One touch |

## Consequences

- Players must assess who requires the most support.
- Who would be the best player to pass to?
- Take advantage of the opponents' strengths/weaknesses.
- Defense: Attack the player with the fewest touches and block the players with the most touches.

## Training objectives

- Adjust to constantly changing basic conditions via varying touch limits.
- Force players to play directly.
- The player receiving a pass must assess and be aware of all passing options even before the ball reaches him.
- Improve awareness and action speed.

# III Possession Soccer

## 6 Introduction

A possession soccer attack is a good choice when possession is gained from an opponent who is formed up and well organized, and a successful counter attack is not possible. The possession attack is characterized by a steady build up and can be made from the wing or the center. The attacking team plays the ball with a series of systematic and steady passes from the defensive third through the midfield into the attacking zone.

The objective of the possession attack is to safeguard possession and to calmly build an attack. The entire team prepares scoring opportunities from the center or the wing with intelligent combinations and coordinated efforts to get open.

## 6.1 Characteristics and tactical rules for a successful possession attack

### Stretching the opposing defensive block
If a counter attack is not possible, it is important to spread out and open up the space to stretch the opposing defensive block, thereby creating more playing space to build up one's own attack.

### Using the entire field in width and depth
Good width and depth coverage on the field is achieved by optimal manning of the sidelines and positioning the forwards as deep as possible. Based on the current offside rule, staying even briefly behind the opposing defensive line in the tactical offside has proven to be an
effective tool.

### Creating a majority near the ball
In order to provide sufficient passing options to the man on the ball and stand up to the opponents' pressing, a majority near the ball should be sought whenever possible.

### Seeking 2 v 1 situations

The 2 v 1 is the smallest possible majority. Horst Wein calls the 2 v 1 scenario the "atom of tactical play." During a possession attack, the team seeks a 2 v 1 majority over any attacking defender as often as possible.

### Creating passing options in every direction

The player in possession of the ball should have as many passing options close to the ball, as well as farther away as possible. He should ideally be able to make long forward or diagonal passes, but also square passes and back passes. However, when passing, the same basic rule applies: depth before width. All players constantly and quickly change their positions according to the game situation, depending on the position of the ball, teammates and opponents.

### Using running feints

In today's soccer, the players are under a huge amount of opposing, spatial, and time pressures. The amount of space around the ball keeps getting smaller. In order to shake off the opponent in these restricted spaces, the use of running feints is indispensable. In doing so, one changes a mental head start into a moving head start.

### Coordinating getting open

Any efforts to get open should always be coordinated. That also applies to the important and effective positional changes in width and depth. When trying to get open, the motto is: create open space and run into open space.

### Forming triangles in every direction

In order to create diagonal passing opportunities and good angles for the man on the ball, triangles must be continuously formed in every direction.

### Taking advantage of gaps

The players run out of the opponent's cover shadow into open areas and quickly man the gaps. In doing so, they take advantage of and man the so-called second gap, the gaps between opponent and teammate. Successful deep play during a possession attack is only made possible by using the lanes and playing the gaps. To have the largest field of vision possible, the players assume a slightly oblique open posture so they can observe the playing area and action and can quickly start another action (dribbling, pass) with the first touch.

### Recognizing passing options before the first touch

The importance of a good first touch as preparation for optimal play cannot be emphasized enough. The player receiving a pass should already be aware of all possible passing options and have made eye contact with a potential pass receiver before making the first touch.

### Anticipating game situations

Today's players are expected to anticipate game situations, quickly grasp them, immediately evaluate (analyze) them, and then make decisions as quickly as possible. We need players who can quickly and effectively adapt to rapidly changing conditions and situations.

### Avoiding risky dribbling in the defensive and middle third

Dribbling in the defensive and middle third should be avoided due to possible loss of possession and resulting threat of a counter attack. In addition, senseless dribbling does not move the opponent's defensive block enough. The ball should be dribbled into open spaces and never into a zone that is loaded with players.

### Achieving a 1 v 1 majority – creating the 1 v 1 challenge

The majority situations against compact defensive blocks can hardly be created with combination play alone. This requires players who have mastered the offensive 1 v 1.

### Mastering group tactics

Mastery of all important group tactics, such as the double pass, playing with a third man, laying off and taking over the ball, crosses and overlapping runs are prerequisites for a successful possession attack.

### Skipping over players or an entire line of players

Skipping over a player or even an entire line of players whenever possible while moving the ball down the field has proven very effective. This means moving downfield quicker with fewer passes.

### Executing a shift in play

To move the opponents' compact defensive block and induce them to make mistakes during a possession attack, the ball must circle quickly and steadily in one's own ranks and shift play from one side to the other. A shift in play is not only a changing of sides with high, long and especially diagonal balls but can also be done with fast passing sequences. The shorter the touch, the less time the opponent has to correct and adjust his position.

### Striving for high execution speed during a shift in play

Applying the principle stop – look – pass, or dribbling, might make it easier to keep the ball in one's own ranks but will not put holes in a well-organized defense. Shifts in play are only successful if they are done quickly and unexpectedly. They must be so fast that the defensive players can no longer correct or insufficiently correct their positions relative to the attackers. Especially effective is a one-time or repeated play in the opposite direction against the opposing shifting formation. The objective of a shift in play is to make a hole either at the wing or in the center to make room for moving the game down the field.

Often a shift in play is necessary during game situations on one of the wings. In these zones, the defending team can easily narrow the game with assistance from the sidelines, put lots of pressure on the attacker on the ball, and block all passing lanes. This greatly increases the threat of a turnover.

Quickly shifting play to the other side can be successful here. The quick change in sides often creates a chance to achieve equal numbers (1 v 1, 2 v 2) or even a majority (2 v 1, 3 v 2) on the other wing. This brief equality or (preferable) majority must then be utilized very quickly by trying to get behind the defense.

### Getting behind the defense

A long diagonal ball behind the defense is especially effective here.

### Getting open the right way

It is very important that every player tries to get open at the right moment and into the right playing zones. The objective with getting open is to gain possession of the ball or to create open space for teammates.

## Changing the pace

It is recommended to occasionally take out the speed and change the rhythm because a tactically strong opponent adjusts to transparent power kicks. Changes in rhythm provide an opportunity for a brief recovery and undermine the opponent's focus.

## Direct Soccer

The fastest way to play the ball is to pass it directly because the ball is simultaneously being controlled and passed. Making two touches to this purpose does not simply require a double effort but also much more time. For this reason, direct passes at the right moment must become a regular component of offensive play if we want to improve our chances at successful offensive play in restricted spaces.

The risk of a turnover must of course be minimized here as well, but without a certain amount of readiness to take a risk in certain situations, a successful attack on a well-organized defense is hardly possible. The foundation of a successful shift in play is a clean passing game over varying distances.

## 6.2    Prerequisites for a successful possession attack

### Technical requirements

- Mastery of all important 1 v 1 and tackling techniques.
- Mastery of all defensive and offensive 1 v 1 techniques.
- The ability to pass quickly, accurately, hard and low over various distances, medium-high or high to a teammate or, make a through pass.
- The ability to make direct plays under lots of pressure and in restricted spaces.
- Optimal control of balls passed at various degrees of hardness and height, to the player or as a through pass.
- Excellent finishing technique with all parts of the foot, especially full instep, outside and inside of the instep, as well as the inside foot.
- The ability to finish with a successful volley (e.g., hip-turn kick, header, etc.) after centering the ball.
- The ability to successfully rebound.

### Tactical requirements

- Understanding of game and tactics
- Playing intelligence
- Keeping track of the game
- The ability to read a game accurately (individually and collectively)
- The ability to anticipate quickly and accurately
- Playing and action speed

- Mastery of a successful shift in play
- The ability to change rhythm
- Mastery of all important group tactics, such as double pass, overlapping runs, crosses, laying off and taking over the ball, playing with a third teammate, skipping a line, etc.
- Mastery of all possession attack features and rules
- Mastery of the offside rule

## Physical requirements

- Speed on and off the ball
- Ingenuity, agility and good coordination, especially in tight spaces,
- Good basic and competition-specific endurance to be able to successfully combine skills and score goals even in the last few minutes of a game
- Strength and assertiveness

## Mental requirements

- Patience
- Self-confidence
- Staying calm on the ball
- Positive aggressiveness
- The ability to perform under pressure
- Distinct desire to win

## Social requirements

- Being a team player and supporting team cohesion
- Cooperativeness
- Responsibility
- A positive attitude

## 6.3    Systematic teaching and practice of a possession attack

From the very start, players must learn the theoretical and practical aspects of basic possession play and attack principles and rules.

Of course, the approach here should also be methodic-didactic:
- From easy to difficult
- From familiar to unfamiliar
- From simple to complex

# 7 Preliminary practice for the possession attack – drill with a third player

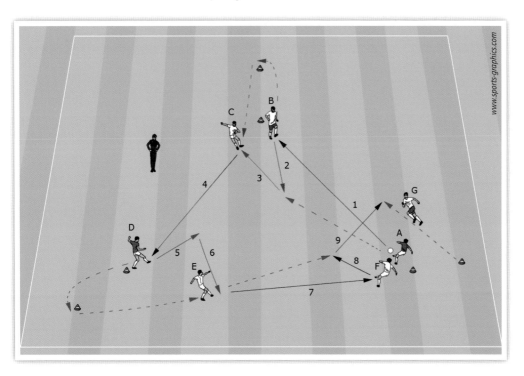

## Progression

A plays to B (1) and runs toward him. B passes back to A (2), crosses to the side and then lines up behind group C. At the right moment, C (the third man) sprints into the open space for the pass from A. A plays a through pass to C (3), sprints to the cone and takes the place of B. C plays direct to D (4) and signals his availability for a wall pass from D. D plays through to C (wall pass) (5), crosses to the back and lines up behind group E. At the right moment, E (third man) sprints into the open space for a pass from C. C plays the ball into the open space to E (6), sprints to the cone and takes the place of D. E plays the ball to F (7) and runs to the next corner of the triangle. F plays a through pass to E (8) and crosses to the back. E plays a through pass to A and takes the place of F (9), etc.

## Tips and suggestions

- During this drill, the players learn and improve the play with a third man and the crossing of two forwards in front of a defensive line.
- Team play and coordinated running patterns of the participating players in particular are being improved here.

# 8    Drills for an improved possession attack

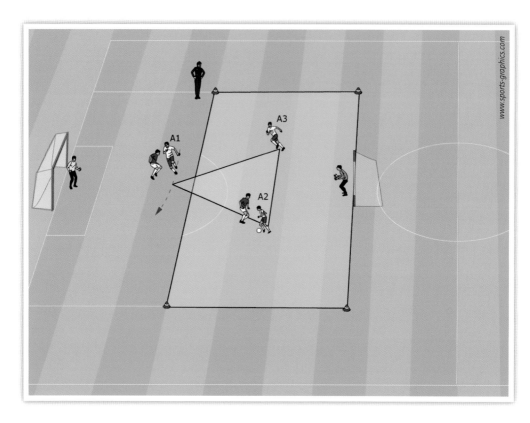

## 3 v 3 on two large goals

Progression

Two teams play 3 v 3, with two large goals with a goalkeeper in a double-sized penalty area.

Variation

- Change the size of the playing field (e.g., 27 yards wide, 38 yards long).

Tips and suggestions

- The triangle formation opens up ideal passing angles and distances for mutual support.
- Create majority situations (3 v 1, 2 v 1, 3 v 2) by using group tactics (double pass, overlapping runs, crossing, laying off and taking over the ball, play with a third man), but also by outplaying the opponent in 1 v 1.

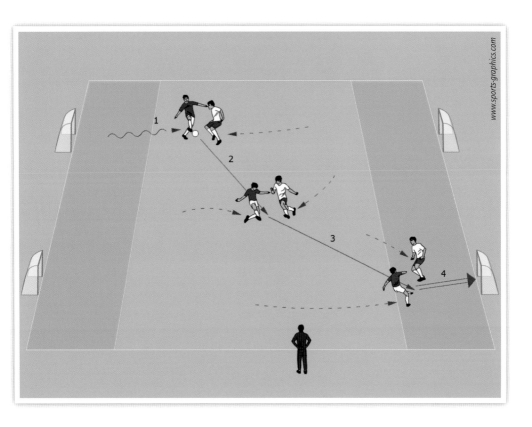

*www.sports-graphics.com*

## 3 v 3 on four small goals

### Progression

Two teams play 3 v 3 on a field (32 x 27 yards) with four small goals. The field is divided into three zones, two end zones (shooting zones) and one middle zone. Goals are only valid if scored from within the shooting zone.

### Tips and suggestions

• The opponents can man only one goal with two players. Therefore, the objective is to achieve a 2 v 1 situation in front of one goal (shift of play, combination play, successful 1 v 1 duels).

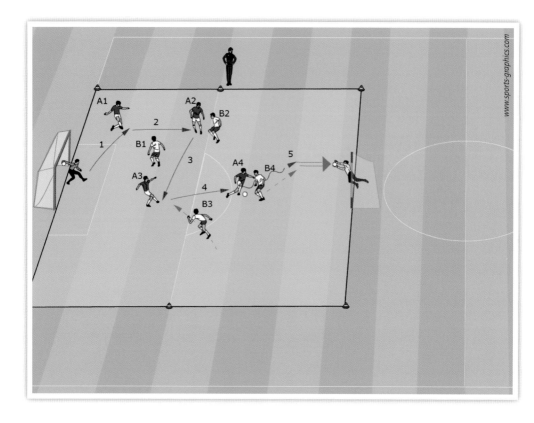

## 4 v 4 on two large goals

Progression
Two teams play 4 v 4 with two large goals and a goalkeeper on a double-sized penalty area.

Tips and suggestions
- Diamond formation when in possession of the ball: this facilitates ideal passing angles and distances and lots of triangles for mutual support.
- Create a majority.
- Skip a line.
- Sensible use of all group tactics.

www.sports-graphics.com

# 4 v 4 on four small goals

## Progression

Play is 4 v 4 on a field (32 x 32 yards) with four small goals. The field is divided into three zones, two shooting zones and one middle zone. Goals are only valid if scored from within the shooting zone.

## Tips and suggestions

- When in possession, use the diamond as basic formation.
- Create majority in front of one goal.
- Use quick shifts in play.

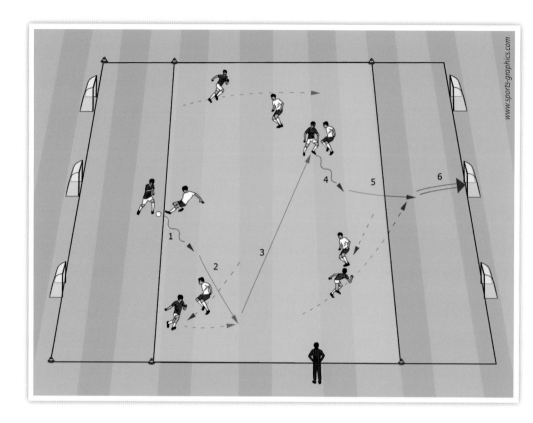

## 5 v 5 on six small goals

### Progression

Two teams play 5 v 5 with six small goals. The field is divided into three zones, two shooting zones and one middle zone. Goals are only valid if scored from within the shooting zone.

### Tips and suggestions

- Good width and depth coverage on the field.
- Use counter-rotating play to constantly change the point of attack.
- Create majority in front of one goal.
- In case of a mini goal shortage, cone goals may be used instead.

### Variations

- Goals are only valid if all players have left their own defensive third.
- Double score for goals scored in the center goals.
- Double score for goals scored in the outside goals.

# 7 v 7 on eight small goals

## Progression

Like the previous drill, but with 7 v 7 on eight mini goals.

## Tips and suggestions

- Good width and depth coverage on the field.
- Use counter-rotating play to constantly change the point of attack.
- Create majority in front of one goal.
- In case of a mini goal shortage, cone goals may be used instead.

## Variations

- Goals are only valid if all players have left their own defensive third.
- Double score for goals scored in the center goals.
- Double score for goals scored in the outside goals.

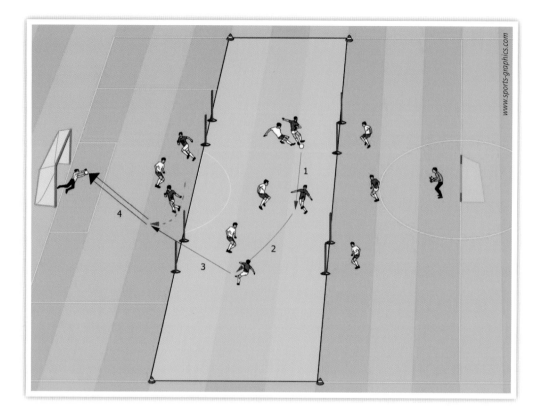

## 7 v 7 through poles on large goals

### Progression

Two teams play 3 v 3 in the middle zone. In the attack zones, play is 2 v 1. Both teams try to play the ball through one of the two cone goals to one of the two forwards. Next, the two forwards finish in a 2 v 1 on the large goal. This is done with a time limit issued by the trainer.

### Variations

- One neutral player in the middle (4 v 3).
- Change goal sizes.
- Three cone goals.
- One defender moves up from the midfield for a 2 v 2.

### Tips and suggestions

- Smart move by one forward to get open (moving down field).
- Quick exploitation of a 2 v 1 majority in the attacking third.

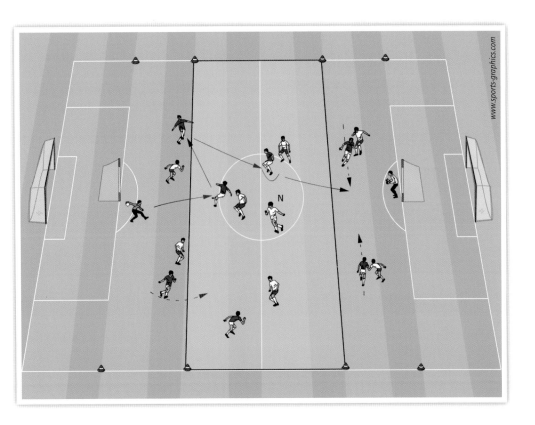

# 8 v 8 + 1 neutral player

## Progression

Play is 8 v 8 from penalty zone to penalty zone with one neutral player in the middle zone. The field is divided into three zones: midfield, opposing end zones. In the midfield, play is 3 v 3 with one neutral player; in the end zones, play is 2 v 2. Goals are only valid if the shot was taken from within the shooting zone.

## Variation

- For the finish, one midfield player can move up for 3 v 2 with time limit.

## Tips and suggestions

- Skillful exploitation of a majority in midfield.
- Smart, coordinated running of forwards.
- Targeted play down field.
- Forceful finish in 2 v 2.

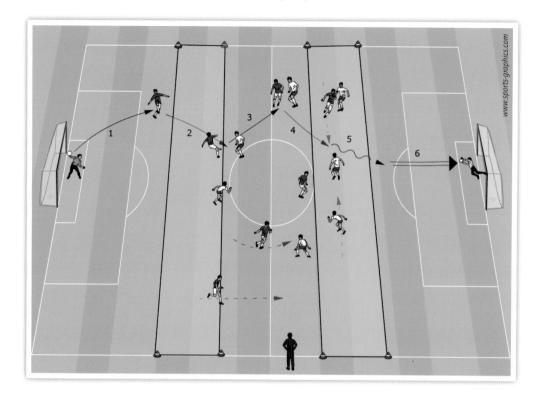

## 8 v 8 – pass into the target zone

### Progression

Two teams play 8 v 8 in the middle zone (field width x 44 yards). When a forward controls a pass in the goal zone (5-10 yards), the attacking team gets one point. However, the ball must reach the goal zone before him. After that, the attacking team has the chance to score another point with a solo run that ends with a goal within 5 seconds.

### Variations

- One defender is allowed to pursue.
- 2 v 1 for the finish.

### Tips and suggestions

- Good width and depth coverage on the field.
- Shift in play – play in opposite directions.
- Well-timed balls into the goal zone.
- Resolute solo-run with finish.

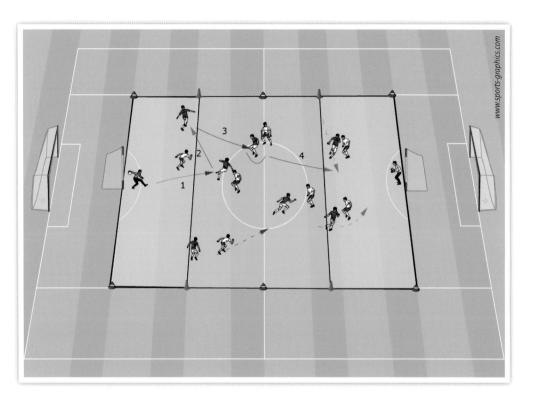

www.sports-graphics.com

## 8 v 8 from penalty box to penalty box without outer zones

### Progression

Play is 8 v 8 on a field, penalty area to penalty area, and the width of the penalty area. Since the width of the field is limited the possession attack is more difficult than it is using the entire field width. The end zone line also serves as the offside line.

### Variations

- A goal is only valid if the entire offensive team has moved completely out of its own defensive third. That means moving up is mandatory.
- 9 v 9
- 10 v 10

### Tips and suggestions

- Good width and depth coverage on field.
- Change positions while moving down field.
- Use running feints.
- Coordinated runs before reaching the offside line.

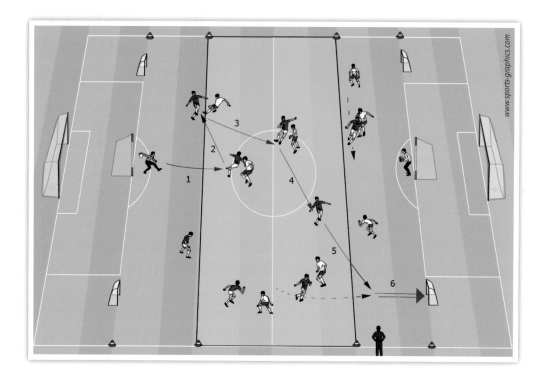

## 9 v 9 on four mini and two large goals

### Progression

Play is 9 v 9 from penalty area to penalty area, with four mini goals and two large goals with goalkeeper. Goals are only valid within the end zone. Players can choose between taking a shot at the large goal with a goalkeeper or one of the mini goals. Goals scored in the large goal get a double score. End zone lines also serve as offside lines.

### Variations

- Goals are only valid if all attacking players have left their own defensive zone.
- 10 v 10
- 11 v 11

### Tips and suggestions

- Good width and depth coverage on field.
- Passes should be deep rather than wide.
- Shift of play.
- Seek majority situations.
- If there are no mini goals available, cone goals can be used for dribbling through.

# 11 v 11 on two large goals – open play

## Progression

Open play, meaning no restriction on number of touches, between two teams 11 v 11 on a regulation size field.

## Players pay attention to the following

- Spread out and open up space.
- Good width and depth coverage on field.
- Create a majority close to the ball.
- Create passing options in all directions.
- Form triangles.
- Change positions across the field and down the field.
- Run into open space and create open space (out of the cover shadow into open areas).
- Play the gaps.
- Optimal first touch.
- Shift in play.

## Final games on two goals

| Guidelines | Goals |
|---|---|
| Limit number of touches | Quickly build up play |
| Limit playing area | Difficulty, increase spatial and opposing pressure |
| Use neutral players | Majority, utilize uneven number of players, promote direct play |
| Timing | Make up advantage, time pressure |
| Inferior number play | Dribbling, 1 v 1 |
| Vary number of goals (four goals, six goals) | Play wide, seek majority |

# IV Wing Play

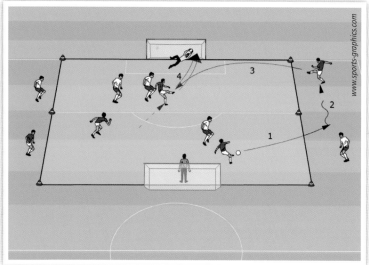

## 3 v 3 + 2 wing players

### Progression

The playing field consists of an inner zone and a wing area. Play in the inner zone is 3 v 3 (with 2-3 touches) and, in the wing area, it is open play. Two players from each team, who may not be attacked, will center the ball and are waiting to spring into action outside in the wing area flush with the centerline. Goals scored after the wing player centered the ball or made a back pass get double points (i.e., triple), goals from the game get single points.

### Variation

- 4 v 4 on the infield.

### Tips and suggestions

- Well-placed wing play.
- Coordinated running after the center and triangle formation.
- Utilize second chance to shoot at the goal (rebound).
- Go to the ball (don't stand where the ball goes).
- Forwards should run to the ball as it is being centered (more difficult to cover, greater vertical leap, more energy for the header or shot on goal).

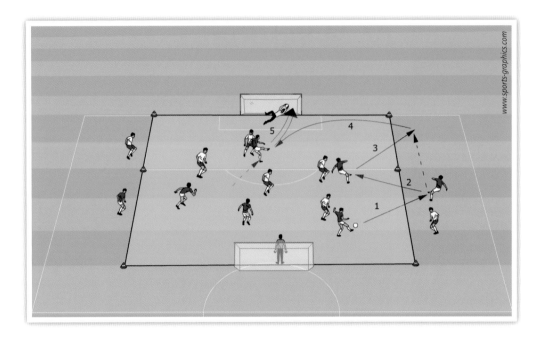

## 5 v 5 on the wing with options

### Progression

Like the previous game, only with additional options: inside and outside players may play together (double passes, overlapping runs, overlap and subsequent play with a third man).

### Variations

- 6 v 6 inside
- 7 v 7 inside

### Tips and suggestions

- Well-placed wing play.
- Coordinated running after center, and triangle formation.
- Utilize second chance to shoot on goal (rebound).

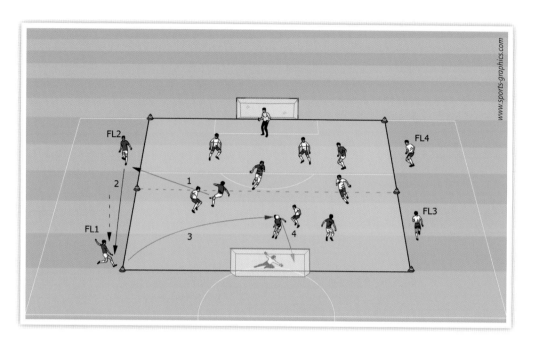

www.sports-graphics.com

## 5 v 5 – play on both goals with neutral goalkeepers

### Progression

Two teams play in both directions with two large goals with neutral goalkeepers. Goals are only valid after a cross or back pass from the neutral outside zone. After gaining possession, the outside zone must be played first. The two outside players from a team are allowed to play in both directions and center the ball for the teammates in front of both goals. If the goalkeeper holds the ball or it goes out of bounds, the goalkeeper throws it to a wing player from the other team. The attackers stay in possession when a goal is scored. A rebound is allowed before the ball must be played back into the wing zone.

### Variations

- 6 v 6 inside
- 7 v 7 inside

### Tips and suggestions

- Well-placed wing play.
- Good teamwork between wing and inside players is a basic requirement for the success of this form of play.
- Possible cross away from the goal and toward the goal.
- Constant changing of formation for the finish.
- Form triangle for finish.

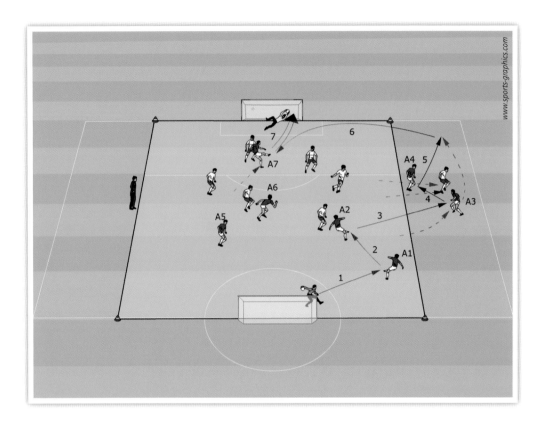

## 7 v 7 – 2 v 1 on the wing

Progression
_____

No more than two attackers and one defender in the outside zone. Goals scored after a center or back pass count double (first or second ball); a headed goal counts triple. Play with or without offside depends on the players' skill level.

Tips and suggestions
_____

- Well-placed wing play.
- Shift in play.
- Effective exploitation of 2 v 1 majority on the wing (overlap, double pass).
- Well-timed centers and back passes.
- Form triangle for finish.

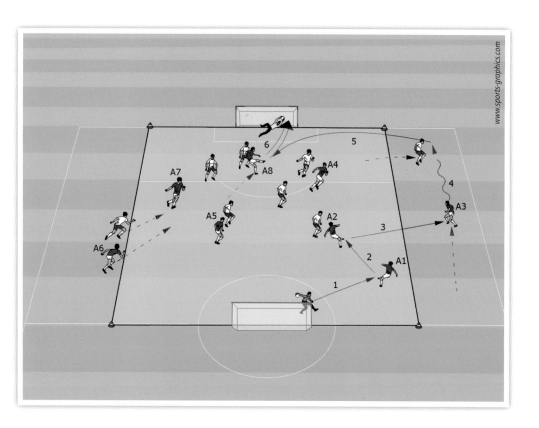

www.sports-graphics.com

## 8 v 8 – two touches inside – open outside

### Progression

Two teams play 8 v 8 on two large goals. The limited number of touches on the inside automatically facilitates wing play.

### Tips and suggestions

- Well-placed wing play.
- Shift in play.
- Seek majority on the wing.
- Goals after a center of back pass count double.

## 7 v 7 – dribbling across the goal line

Progression

Play is 7 v 7 on a field (width of field x 55 yards). Each team plays with three goals. The outside goals are larger than the goals in the middle to motivate the players to play along the outside. Dribbling through the goal in the center earns the team one point. Dribbling through the wing goals is rewarded with two points.

Tips and suggestions

- Good width and depth coverage on field.
- Shift in play.
- Well-placed wing play.

## 8 v 8 – pass into the target zone

### Progression

Two teams play 8 v 8 on the entire field. The attacking team gets one point if a forward controls a pass into the target zone. However, the ball must reach the target zone before him. After that, the attacking team has a chance to earn another point by scoring a goal after a cross to two running forwards.

### Variation

• One defensive player is allowed to penetrate the end zone to keep the forwards from finishing.

### Tips and suggestions

• Good width and depth coverage on field.
• Shift in play.
• Well-timed balls into the target zone.
• Well-placed wing play.
• Ball accurately centered for two crossing forwards.

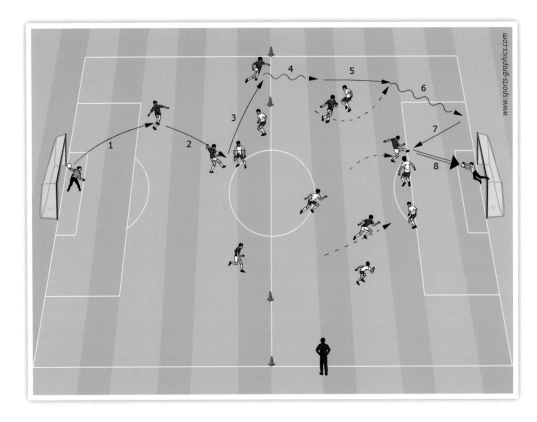

## 8 v 8 – play through the wing goals

### Progression

Two teams play 8 v 8 on the entire field. They can only play across the centerline if a player dribbles through a wing goal on the outside or passes to a teammate. Another option is a player sprints through the cone goal and catches a diagonal pass played from his side of the field. This pass does not have to be played through the wing goals.

### Tips and suggestions

- The rule induces the players to play the wings.
- Shift in play.
- Fast dribble.
- Well-timed diagonal passes.

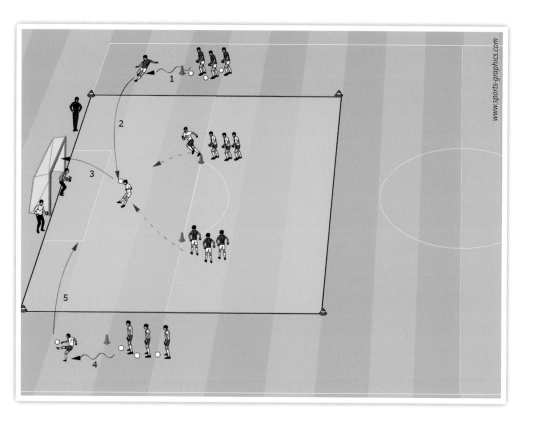

## Competition – goal after a cross

### Progression

Two teams compete in a cross-finish shooting contest, alternating left and right. Who converts the most crosses? The scorer retrieves the ball and lines up with the crossing players on his team. The player who crossed the ball lines up behind the scorers from his team. A header goal earns a team three points, a direct shot into the goal earns two points, and a goal after a pass earns one point. After 8-10 minutes, teams switch sides so everyone gets to cross once from the left and once from the right.

### Tips and suggestions

- The goal scorer does rush off but rather waits until he has properly calculated and assessed the trajectory. Important: balls that are too long are lost; a ball that is too short can be run down.
- The goal scorers should always run to the ball to finish with a harder shot.
- Individual competition: who scores the most goals? Each player plays a round in all four positions.
- After an action, the players are careful not to get into the line of fire of one of the opposing teams' players.

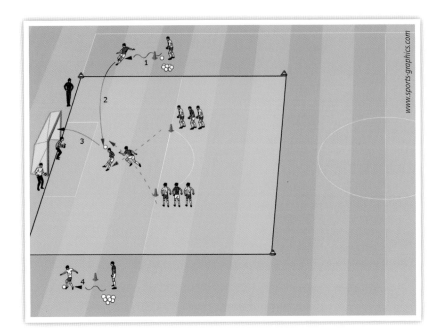

## Shot at the goal after crossover

### Progression

Two players run to their cones at the penalty area boundary line. When they get there, they have three options: cross over, stop the crossover, or no crossover and utilize the subsequent cross. Which team scores the most goals? Header goal is worth three points, otherwise direct conversion is worth two points, and goals with two touches are worth one point.

### Variations

- Free kick cross
- A 1-2 cross (assist, cross)
- Cross from a dribble
- Use of defenders
- Which group of three scores the most goals?

### Tips and suggestions

- The crosses are short or long, either into free space or to a specific (previously determined) player.
- Who decides if a crossing over should be aborted? The player standing at the second post not only sees the cross but also a change of running direction by his partner. The back player thus reacts to the front player. If the back player wants to break off a cross, he must give the front player an audible signal so he can react accordingly.

# V  Shooting at the Goal

## 9  Introduction

The most exciting and suspenseful moments in a soccer game clearly take place around the goal box when a goal is scored. Soccer has changed and will continue to change. The speed of all playing actions will continue to get faster. The area around the ball will be blocked more effectively. Every technique must be mastered and executed accurately under pressure with tremendous speed, today and in the future. Therefore, the demands made on our players for a successful finish continue to grow. This trend in soccer must also be taken into consideration during shooting practice.

Modern shooting practice should be motivating and realistic. Small competitions and drills incorporating pressure of space, opponent, group, and accuracy are perfectly suited for this.

### 9.1  Numbers, data, and facts

- According to Doucet, a team executes between 230 and 280 offensive actions per game. Of those, 5-25 are considered dangerous and effective. Teams average 1.5 goals per game, meaning that it takes approximately 150 offensive actions to score one goal.
- Breakdowns from world and European cup games show that approximately 90% of all goals in a game are scored from within the penalty box.
- Of those, 59% are head-on in front of the goal, between the goal and penalty box boundary line, and most of these between the goal box and the penalty mark.
- Most assists /final passes are also made from the penalty box.
- Many assists come after a cross or back pass from the wing.
- The long-range shot is primarily used by free kick specialists. Otherwise, relatively few goals are scored from longer distances.
- Most goals are scored after a volley or with a second touch. This makes the technical perfection of the direct shot and perfect ball control with the first touch a vital objective of modern shooting practice.
- One in six goals scored is a header.
- Many goals are scored after stray balls and ricochets.

- Technical execution is situation-dependent and varies between inside instep, full instep, inside and outside of the foot.
- The accurate, perfectly timed final pass is a prerequisite to most successfully scored goals.

## 9.2    Two types of training for shooting at the goal

- Practice of shooting technique
- Competition-like shooting practice.

Both forms of practice are important for all performance levels. However, the higher the players' skill level, the more important shooting practice is under realistic conditions. Even top players acquire the necessary accuracy for a shot at the goal through regular repetition of basic shooting techniques.

## 9.3    Technical training for shooting at the goal

In shooting practice, age-appropriate and tested drills lay the foundation for a successful finish. Players learn and improve all of the important shooting techniques after dribbling, controlling the ball, and direct play through lots of repetition. They learn to accurately assess the ball's trajectory and to move their bodies into the ideal shooting position. The trainer designs drills that allow him to teach important finishing techniques in the most effective way. A well-organized drill sequence is essential so the players achieve the necessary number of repetitions. The trainer should absolutely avoid long waits (in line) for the next shooting opportunity.

### Beginners learn...
- to kick the stationary ball directly into the goal
- to take a well-aimed shot into the goal from a dribble
- to convert throw-ins with foot or head

### Advanced
- Practice shots out of a turn after a sprint to the ball or from a jump.
- Use a series of different techniques.
- Aadapt constantly to the ball's changing speed and height.

Drills to improve shooting technique vary from competition-like shooting practice largely because they are done without interactions with opponents.

## 9.4    Training the shot at the goal in a realistic setting

The best shooting technique is worthless if the player isn't able to successfully convert a ball in a difficult situation under the greatest spatial, opposing and time pressures. Competition-like shooting practice must therefore simulate competitive pressure as much as possible. Drills in restricted spaces that constantly alternate between offensive and defensive actions are ideal for this purpose. Here, the players learn to react at lightning speed, to anticipate or sense (the player with a nose for a goal), to prepare, and to utilize scoring opportunities. Drills in the double penalty box, for instance, are also a perfect way to train and improve the action speed that is so fundamental to soccer and the successful finish. Shooting contests with two or more teams competing against each other are also very motivating for the players. The pressure for accuracy and group pressure generated here also produce a competition-like atmosphere.

## 9.5    Conclusions to training the shot at the goal

- Modern shooting practice today and in the future should increasingly incorporate drills in and around the penalty area.
- It is recommended to practice shooting and shooting drills in the penalty area.
- Direct shots and goals scored with the second touch from every important position and from various passes should be practiced over and over again.
- Pressure of space, opponent, time and accuracy in drills must increase incrementally in accordance with age and current performance level.
- Small shooting contests lead to a higher motivation level and are more important and have a higher training effect than ever before. Group pressure greatly increases the competitive atmosphere and the fun factor.
- Simple fundamental forms of shooting practice do still have a right to exist. They still are a great way to practice and improve basic shooting techniques with corrections from the trainer.
- The rebound is becoming increasingly important.

## 9.6    Tips and recommendations for training the shot at the goal

- Accuracy over power.
- Lose the opponent with running feints.
- Practice and demand direct shots often.
- Take shots from different directions and angles.
- A variety of passes from all different areas.
- Well-timed runs into the danger zone.
- Don't wait for the ball, but go to the ball.

- Demand and facilitate shooting with both feet (time-saving).
- Encourage the players to use seamless shooting techniques.
- Pay attention to staggered formation in front of the goal.
- Accurate shots from close proximity and aimed at the corners of the goal.
- Long hard shots into the corners.
- Use disguised shots.
- When doing a solo-run at the goal, use shooting feints to tempt the goalkeeper into premature action.
- Aim for the goalkeeper's week corner (most often his left side).
- The lob is a good choice when the goalkeeper is too far outside the goal.
- The goalkeeper and his position should be registered but this should not distract from the actual objective, the corners of the goal. Target the corners, not the goalkeeper.
- All drills include rebounds for a successful finish.

## 9.7 Training principles

- Complete warm-up as optional preparation.
- No shooting practices when tired.
- Short break between individual shots.
- Always try to shoot with both feet.
- Lots of repetitions.
- Constructive feedback – correction – and praise.
- From easy to difficult.
- From familiar to unfamiliar.
- From simple to complex.
- Training should be versatile; avoid boredom.
- Maintain a healthy balance between workload and recovery.

## 9.8 Tips for shooting practice organization, structure, and methodology

- Make sure you have plenty of balls on hand. There should be at least one ball per player.
- Form small groups for plenty of repetitions and to avoid long waits.
- Portable goals are very helpful.
- Shooting practice does not have to be skipped if no goalkeeper is available. Field players can alternate as goalkeepers.

- Handball or mini goals, or marking cones may also be used.
- Have plenty of multi-colored pinnies on hand for practice drills.
- Always have enough extra balls in the goal for practice drills.
- Regularly switch wall players and neutrals.

## 9.9    Different types of shots at the goal

- We categorically differentiate between the following types of shots:
- Inside foot kick
- Instep kick
- Inside instep kick
- Outside instep kick
- Dropkick
- Hip swivel
- Sideways scissor kick
- Bicycle kick
- Kicks with the toe (toe kick) or the heel (back-heel kick)
- Header

### 1. Inside foot kick

The most often used technique for putting the ball in the corners of the goal because of the large target area near the goal, but also as a lob over the goalkeeper from mostly shorter distances.

### 2. Instep kick

The instep kick produces the hardest shots and the highest velocity. It is used for the free kick, penalty kick, volleys, clearing a ball, a punt by the goalkeeper, and as a lob over the goalkeeper.

### 3. Inside instep kick

The inside instep kick is the most often used shooting technique, especially for long distances, crosses, corners and free kicks.

### 4. Outside instep kick

Unlike passing, shooting with the outside instep is less relevant but should be mastered. In some exceptional cases, the outside instep kick can be the easier and more promising choice. The necessary hardness can be generated immediately after an assist and especially as a dropkick.

### 5. Dropkick

In a game, the dropkick is used as a punt by the goalkeeper when clearing a ball from the defensive zone for a shot at the goal.

### 6. Hip swivel

The hip swivel is a very complex movement and requires good coordination and timing, and extremely flexible hip joints. It facilitates well-placed and hard volleys at the goal.

### 7. Sideways scissor kick

The sideways scissor kick is similar in execution to the hip swivel. But unlike the hip swivel, the player is sideways in the air.

### 8. Bicycle kick

The bicycle kick is by far the most complicated and spectacular technical move in soccer. While falling backwards with his back to the goal, the player kicks the ball, which is higher than his head, with the instep from a horizontal position. It begins with a shearing motion. The bicycle kick is not without danger, especially on artificial turf. It is recommended that beginners practice on a gym mat.

### 9. Kicks with the toe or the heel

Toe kicks at the goal are often used under time pressure and very suddenly. Occasionally goals are scored with heel kicks with the back to the goal.

### 10. Header

The header is and will continue to become more important offensively and defensively. In addition to the technique, a powerful leap, the necessary ruggedness for the aerial duel, and timing all are important factors.

We differentiate between:

- Headers from a standing position (jump with both feet)
- Headers at a run (one-legged jump)
- Headers with and without a twist (standing/running)
- Diving header

# 10  Technical Training for the Shot at the Goal

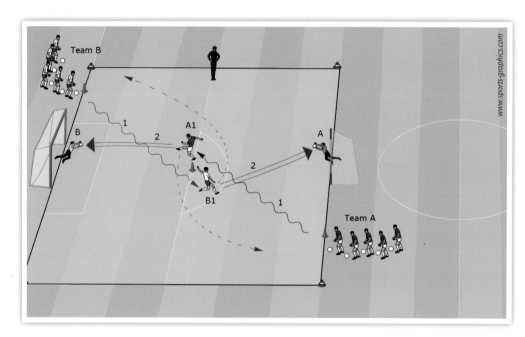

## Shot at the goal after dribbling

### Progression

Players from team A and team B take turns shooting at the goal after a brief dribble from the double penalty area (1-4). Goals are only valid if the shot was taken from the penalty mark. A player from the other team retrieves the ball. Goalkeeper A belongs with team A. Each player has 5-10 shots. Which team will score the most goals? The competitive atmosphere creates lots of pressure for accuracy, as well as group pressure.

### Variations

- Start from the right and the left side.
- Distance of 20-22 yards.
- Possible rebound.

### Tips and suggestions

- If there are too many players, the trainer should form three groups and hold a scrimmage competition. The group taking a break has to perform an additional task.
- Demand a two-footed finish from different shooting angles.
- Use varying shooting techniques (inside foot, inside instep, full instep, outside foot).

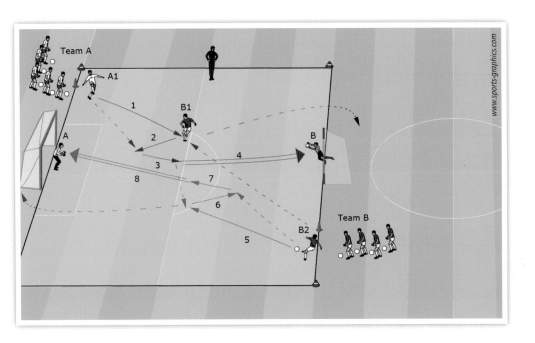

## Shot at the goal with the second touch

### Progression

A pass from A1 to B1 (1). B1 lets it bounce off to A1 (2) and runs back to his own group. A1 must finish with two touches (trap, shoot). Afterward, A1 lets the pass from B2 bounce off, etc.

### Variations

- Start from the right and the left side.
- Distance of 20-22 yards.
- Possible rebound.

### Tips and suggestions

- The player moves diagonally with the ball and prepares for the finish with the first touch.
- Each player has 5-10 shots. Which team scores the most goals?
- The competitive atmosphere creates lots of pressure for accuracy, as well as group pressure.

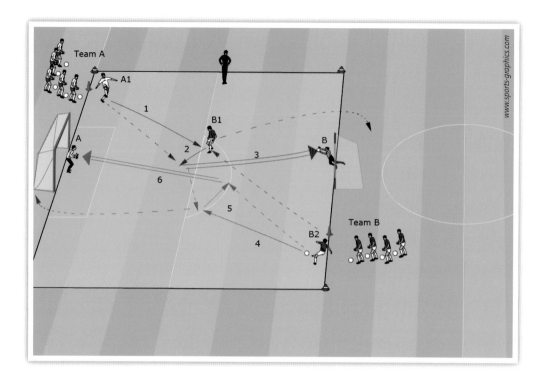

## Shot at the goal after give and go

### Progression

Pass from A1 to B1 (1). B1 plays diagonally to A1 (2) and runs back to his own group. A1 takes a direct shot at the goal. Afterward, A1 immediately takes the position of passing player for B2, etc.

### Variations

- Start from the right and the left side.
- Distance of 20-22 yards.
- Possible rebound.

### Tips and suggestions

- The give and go player does a running feint just before his teammate passes him the ball.
- The give and go player puts the ball precisely into the running path of his teammate, who finishes with a direct shot.

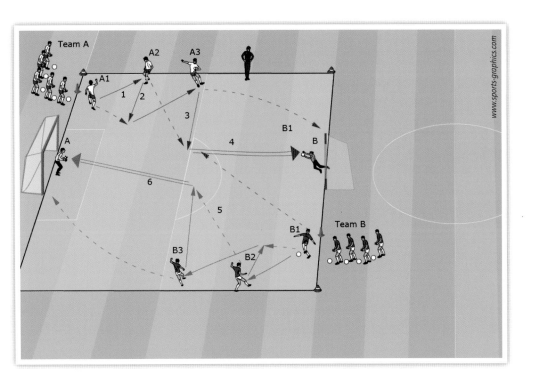

## Shot at the goal by the third man

### Progression

A1 and B1 simultaneously pass to A2 and B2 (1). The wall players (A2 and B2) let the ball drop off the chest and run to the finish (2). A1 and B1 play long passes to A3 and B3. At the same time, A1 and B1 run to the ball (3). A3 and B3 let the ball drop off to the approaching A2 and B2 (4), who go for the finish (5). A3 and B3 retrieve the ball and line up on the opposite side (never-ending format). All players move to the next position (A1 to A2 and A2 to A3).

### Variations

- Skip one player – A1 plays immediately to A3, who passes to A2 as before.
- Contest for time and the run back to the own team. Who scores the most goals?

### Tips and suggestions

- Accurate passing game.
- Situational hardness of passes.
- Final pass is a well-timed through pass.
- Use running feints.

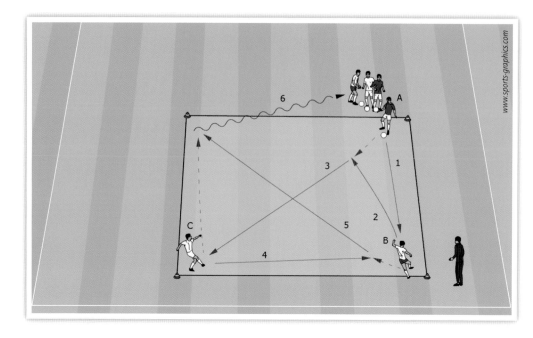

# Direct soccer in a square – preliminary practice

### Progression

Direct play in a square is a drill for 5-8 players and flows as a never-ending exercise. The basic passing sequence is: forward – back – diagonal – sideways – long (into the running path of the last player). Each player completes two actions (passes) before moving to the next station (clockwise). The last player dribbles back to the group's starting point. A plays to B (1) and briefly signals his availability moving sideways. B plays back to A (2) and signals his availability for a wall pass with C. A plays diagonally to C (3) and afterward takes B's position. C plays diagonally to B (4) and runs to the next cone. B plays a through pass to C (5) and takes C's position. C controls the ball and dribbles to the back of his group.

### Variations

- Vary the size of the square (9 x 9 yards to 22 x 22 yards).
- Practice in both directions – clockwise and counter-clockwise – and apply the principle of two-footed play.

### Tips and suggestions

- Players should execute all tactical-technical actions with both feet so they won't lose precious time in a game by avoiding the weak foot.
- This drill is prep for the following shooting exercise and is ideal for the second warm-up phase.

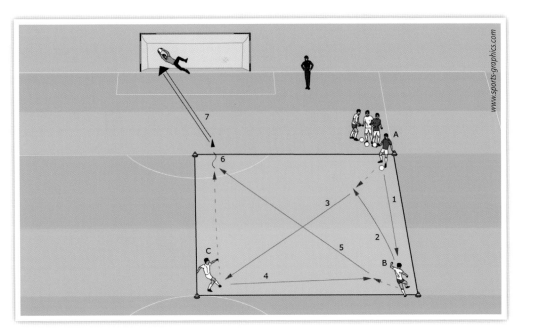

# Direct soccer in a square with shot at the goal

### Progression

A plays to B (1) and briefly signals his availability by moving sideways. B plays back to A (2) and signals his availability for a wall pass with C. A plays diagonally to C (3) and subsequently takes B's position. C plays sideways to B (4) and runs to the next cone. B plays a through pass to C (5) and takes C's position. C controls the ball and finishes with a goal (6).

### Variations

- Frequently change the size of the square so players must constantly adapt to new distances. This will help them develop a better feel for different passes and distances.
- Practice in both directions (clockwise/counter-clockwise).
- If the starting point is on the left, the shooter should practice primarily with his right foot. If you want to practice shooting with the left foot, run the exercise in mirror reverse. The starting point will be on the right.

### Tips and suggestions

- Use running feints and running approach.
- Clean passing game.
- The better the last pass is played into the space or into the running path of the attacker, the more promising the finish. The final pass must be timed so the shooter can reach it without having to slow down.

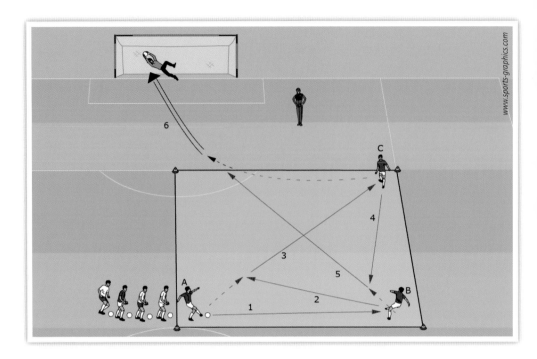

## Direct soccer in a square – 90° shot at the goal

### Progression

Like the previous shooting drill, but now the starting point is in the diagonally opposite corner. The task for players within the same cycle as the previous drill changes when the passing sequence rotates 90°. Then the starting point for the drill is in the diagonally opposite corner.

### Tips and suggestions

- The shooter does not run vertically to the goalkeeper but rather parallel to the 18-yard line (he crosses to an imaginary defense line). This facilitates practicing shots from a turn.
- If the starting point is on the left, the shooter practices with the right foot. If you want to practice shooting with the left foot, run the exercise in mirror reverse. The starting point will be on the right.

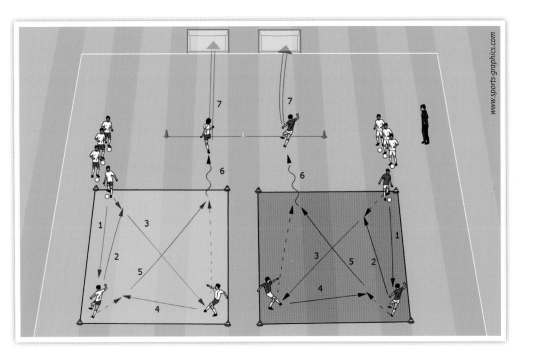

# Direct soccer in a square – competition

## Progression

If this drill is run as a competition, players will experience time pressure and pressure to play with accuracy. After briefly controlling the ball, players finish the learned passing sequence with a shot at a mini goal from outside the shooting zone (6). The distance to the mini goals depends on the players' performance level. The shooter retrieves his ball from the goal and lines up behind the last player from his team. Each team runs one time from both the left and right side. Goals scored will be added up.

The team that scores the most goals within a certain amount of time wins the competition.

## Variations

- Players shoot at one large goal with a goalkeeper from the opposing team.
- Shot at the goal must be direct.

## Tips and suggestions

- Accuracy over speed! The objective is to make clean passes or take clean shots in spite of the intense time pressure (pressure for accuracy).
- Each team runs one time from both the left and right side. Goals scored will be added up.
- Players learn to maintain a balance between speed and accuracy (accuracy over speed!) because they want to be able to score as many goals as possible and win the game.

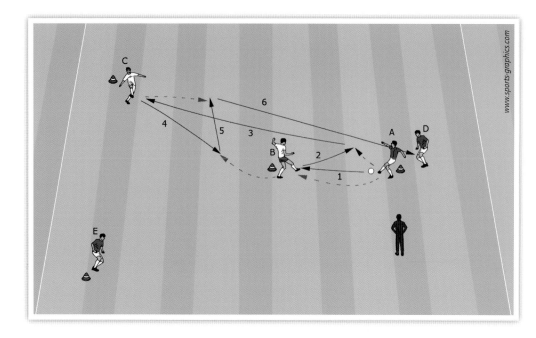

## Y-drill – endless as preliminary practice

### Progression

A plays to B and signals his availability for a wall pass, moving sideways (1). B plays a through pass to A and signals his availability for a pass from C (2). A plays direct to C and takes B's position (3). C plays a wall pass with B (4, 5). C plays direct to E (6) who continues the drill on the left side with D. All players move to the next position.

### Variation
- Skip one player (A passes right to C, etc.).

### Tips and suggestions
- Quick and (preferably) direct passing game.
- The trainer watches for accuracy and situational hardness of passes.
- Players use running feints, coordinate their running efforts, and coach each other.
- The drill is executed on both sides to factor in the principle of two-footed play.

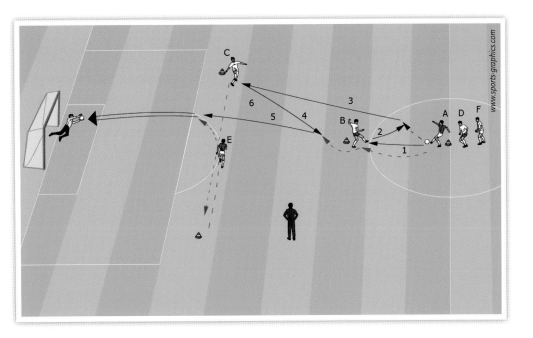

## Y-drill – cutting across with a shot at the goal

### Progression

This is a combination play with two midfielders and two forwards. The two forwards cut across in front of the defenders. As they cut across, their running paths depend on the game situation and defenders' actions. A plays to B and signals his availability for a wall pass, moving sideways (1). B plays a through pass to A and signals his availability for a pass from C (2). A plays direct to C (3) and takes B's position. C lets the ball drop off and crosses with D (4). B plays a long pass into the running path of D (5), who finishes with a goal (6). All players move to the next position and D retrieves the ball.

### Variations

- The drill is performed the same way from the left side with player D. This forces the players to practice equally with both feet. Playing from the right side trains primarily the right foot, from the left side the left foot.
- The starting player (A) skips one line and passes directly to position C.

### Tips and suggestions

- Use running feints.
- Players coach each other.
- Coordinated runs, especially when cutting across.
- Drill is done from both sides to factor in the principle of two-footed play.

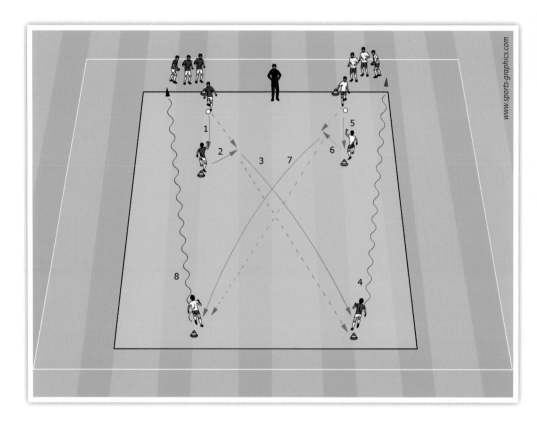

## Direct soccer figure-8 – basic preparatory pattern

### Progression

Wall pass (1, 2), followed by a low diagonal push pass (3). The receiving player controls the ball and dribbles to the group on the right. Next, the first player from the next group begins the same sequence on the right side (5-8). After making their pass, all players move to the next station. A minimum of 8-10 players is needed for this drill.

### Tips and suggestions

- The trainer makes sure that the starting player begins wall play as quickly as possible. The second group starts immediately after player B has run through the center.
- Use running feints.
- Accurate, hard passes.
- Players coach each other.

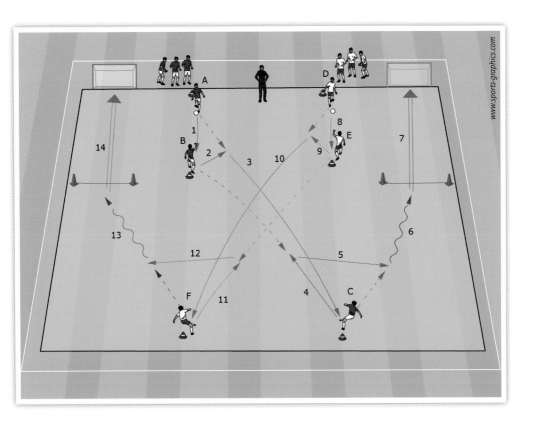

# Direct soccer figure-8 – competition with a shot at the goal

## Progression
Progresses like the previous drill. C controls the ball and dribbles to the shooting line (6). At the shooting line, he finishes with a shot at the mini goal (7). The trainer makes sure that the starting players from the other group begin wall play as quickly as possible. Thus, the second group starts (here: player D) as soon as player B has run through the center. Each player always moves to the next position.

## Variations
- Shot at the large goal with goalkeeper.
- Depending on the performance level, the goal may be placed closer or farther away.

## Tips and suggestions
- The smaller the goals and the longer the distance, the more pressure on the players for accuracy.

# 11    Shooting Competitions

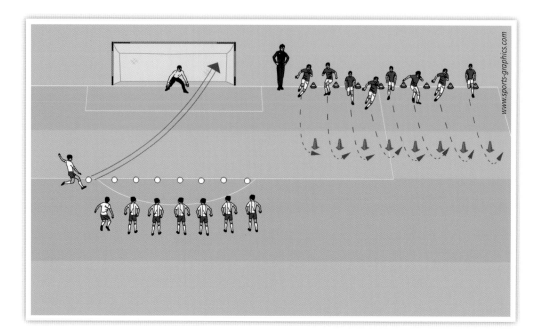

## At the goal or group run

### Progression

Two teams play each other. Team A takes a shot at the goal and team B stands at the goal line next to the cones. If a player from team A misses the goal, the entire team A must run around the goal before the next player can take his turn. If the goalkeeper saves the ball or it hits the post/crossbar, the next player from team A takes a shot. If the ball goes in the goal, team B has to run around the markings. After a predetermined amount of time (e.g., 2-3 minutes), the teams switch tasks. Who scores the most goals?

### Variations

- Vary the running distances (6-18 yards).
- Vary the shooting distance (12 yards, 18 yards, 22 yards).
- Varied execution (stationary ball, brief pass to self with shot at the goal, shot at the goal from a dribble).

### Tips and suggestions

- Shots at the goal are only allowed when the goalkeeper is ready.
- High group pressure during the shot at the goal.
- High performance pressure during the shot at the goal if many shots miss the goal.

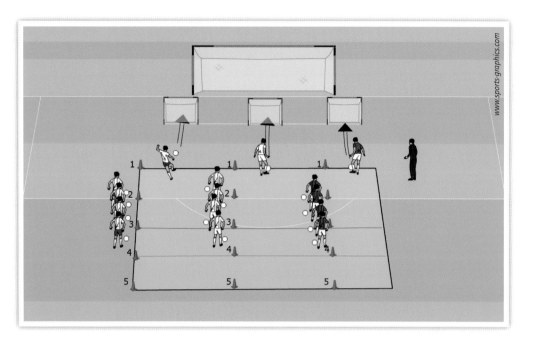

www.sports-graphics.com

# Champions League 1

### Progression

In this drill, players take shots at mini goals. Whoever scores moves up. Whoever misses moves down or stays in his league. Each cone stands for a performance class, from the local league to the champions' league. The first player to put the ball in the goal from the champions' league cone is the winner.

### Variations

- The number of cones and the number of leagues can vary. (Example: local league, state league, regional league, national B league, national A league, champions' league)
- Group competitions.

### Tips and suggestions

- Set distances according to players' performance level.
- Form as many groups as possible to avoid repetition.
- Demand different shooting techniques.

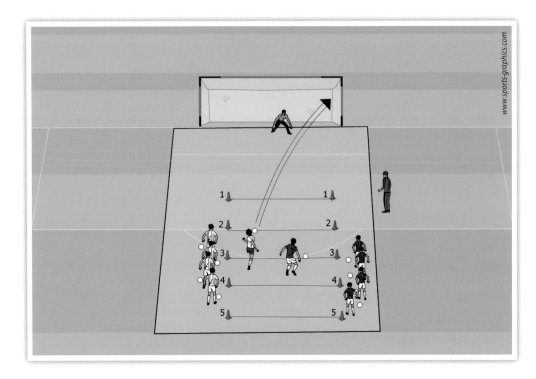

## Champions League 2

### Progression

This is the champions' league version with one large goal and a goalkeeper. Cones are set up at distances of 12, 17, 19, and 22 yards. Each player starts at the first cone. Whoever scores moves to the next cone. The first player to put the ball in the goal from the farthest cone is the winner.

### Variations

- Group competition.
- Shoot after dribbling.

### Tips and suggestions

- Distances of cones and thus the degree of difficulty should be set according to players' performance level.
- Two goalkeepers take turns so the shots can be taken in more rapid succession.
- If there are too many players (more than 12), two goals should be used.

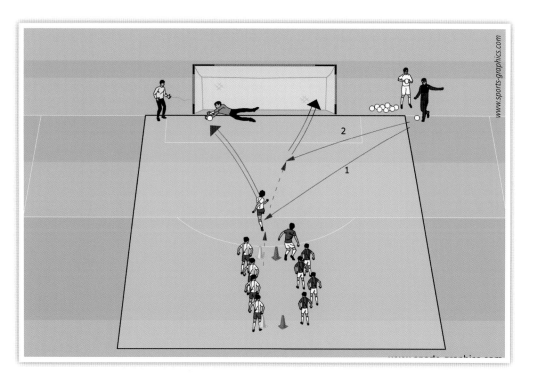

## Challenge

### Progression

Two teams with 5-8 players each play a team competition. The trainer or an assistant rapidly passes two balls to each player. The first pass is played into a zone near the penalty mark, the second, immediately after the shot at the goal, approximately 7-9 yards in front of the goal. A player who converts one ball can line up again at the back of his group and is still in the game. A player who misses both shots is out of the game and helps to pass the missed balls to the trainer. If a player scores with both balls, he can challenge a player (usually the best player) on the other team. This player then has to absolutely put both balls in the goal or he is out of the game.

### Variation

- The shooting distance can be changed according to the players' performance level.

### Tips and suggestions

- It would be best to use two goalkeepers.
- If there are too many players, the trainer should organize a tournament with four teams.
- Pressure on the challenged player is huge.
- This is good practice for the goalkeeper as well because most goals are scored from short distances.

# 12    Shooting practice in a realistic setting

## 3 v 2 + 2 v 3

### Progression

Three attackers and two defenders are in each of the two halves of a double penalty area. The players are not allowed to leave their half. When the ball is played across the centerline, the three attackers have 8 seconds (or less, depending on the level) to score a goal. The goalkeeper is allowed to play directly with the attackers. Goals can be scored from anywhere.

### Variations

- 3 v 1 + 1 v 3 (beginners)
- 2 v 1 + 1 v 2
- 4 v 3 + 3 v 4

### Tips and suggestions

- Position-oriented instruction – specialists (forwards/midfielders/defenders) play against each other.
- Set time limit for the finish in the attacking half.
- Quick play down field after gaining possession.

## 3 v 3 in a double 18-yard box

### Progression

Two teams play 3 v 3 with two goalkeepers in a double penalty area with two large goals.

### Variations

- 4 v 4
- 5 v 5
- Goals from the own half count double.
- Goals after a double pass count double.

### Tips and suggestions

- Triangle formation.
- Use group-based tactics (double pass, overlap, crossing over, play with the third man, lay-off and takeover).
- Create and utilize majority situations (seek 2 v 1).

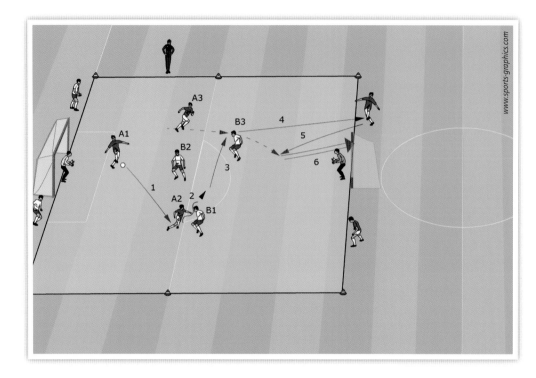

# 3 v 3 + 4 players behind the goal line

## Progression

Two teams play 3 v 3 with two goalkeepers on a double penalty area with two large goals. Two teammates support their team behind each opposing goal. They play directly or with two touches.

## Variations

- 4 v 4
- 5 v 5
- Goals from their own half count double.
- Goals after a back pass from a wing player count double.

## Tips and suggestions

- Quickly move the ball down field after gaining possession.
- Move up for triangle formation.
- Use rebounds.

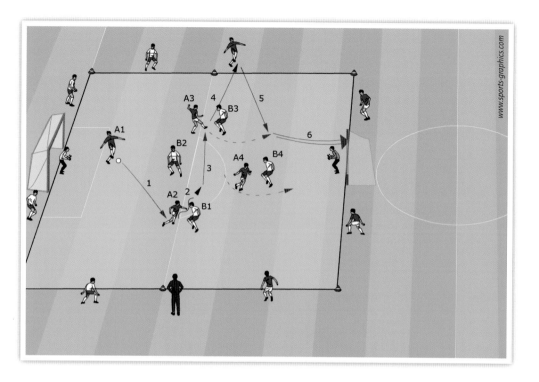

# 4 + 4 v 4 + 4

## Progression

Play is 4 v 4 on a double penalty area. Each team has an additional four players outside their attack zone, two behind the goal and two at the sidelines. Limited number of touches inside and outside, depending on the training objective and performance level.

## Variations

- Long shots from their own half count double.
- Inside and outside players switch positions.

## Tips and suggestions

- Use neutral players in the center (in case of uneven number of players).
- Play down field.
- Move up.
- Triangle formation.
- Play with the third man.
- Well-aimed crosses and back passes from the wings.
- Rebound.

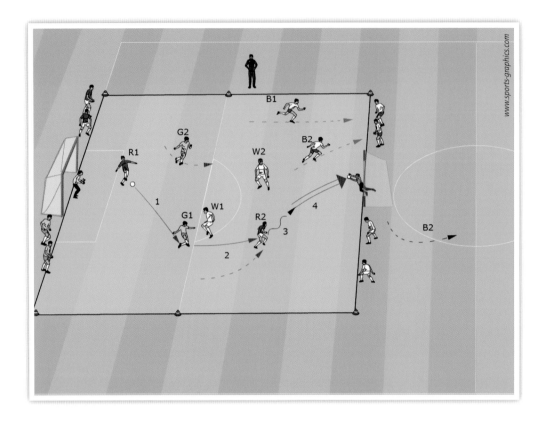

## 4 v 4 with four colors

### Progression

The trainer assembles four groups of two players each with four different colors. Red and gray, as well as blue and white, form a team. The first pair of each color is on the playing field. Play is 4 v 4. The trainer calls a color (e.g., blue). The pair B3/B4 can only enter the field after B1/B2 has exited. The team blue/white is therefore briefly in the minority. The pair red/gray must now quickly take advantage of the situation.

### Tips and suggestions

- The team with the majority must quickly utilize the brief advantage and score a goal.
- The different colors and the constant change between equal, majority and minority numbers improve perceptual and action speed.

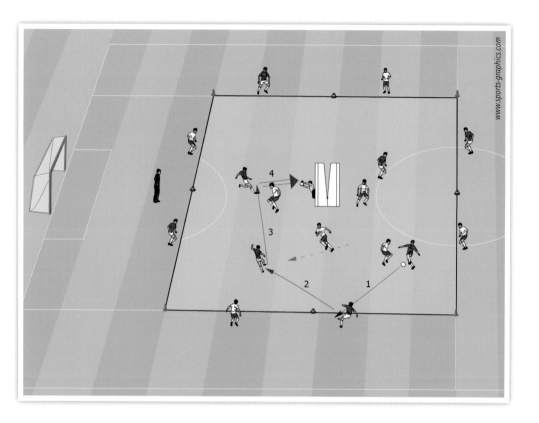

## 4 + 4 v 4 + 4 with back-to-back goals

### Progression

In the center of a square/rectangle (44 x 44 yards) two large goals with goalkeepers are set up back to back. Two teams play 4 v 4 on the inside field. Four additional players from each team are positioned on the outside. Play is open on the inside; on the outside is a two-touch limit. Inside and outside players are allowed to shoot on both goals.

### Variations

- 5 v 5 inside
- 6 v 6 inside

### Tips and suggestions

- Fast changeover from defense to offense, and vice versa.
- Accurate shots from all distances.
- Anticipate shooting opportunities.
- Shots at the goal and crosses from wing players.

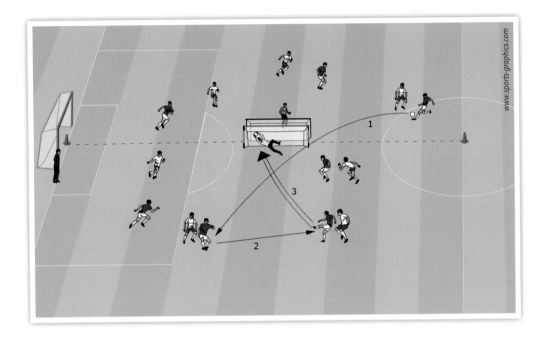

## 7 v 7 with back-to-back goals

### Progression

Two goals are set up back to back in the center of the field (e.g., half of a playing field). Two teams play 7 v 7 with neutral goalkeepers. Both teams can score on both goals. When a goal is scored, the goalkeeper throws out the ball to the farthest player on the scoring team. If the goalkeeper saves a goal, the other team gets the ball (long throw-out).

### Variations

- 8 v 8 (9 v 9)
- Goals on only one designated side with a designated goalkeeper.
- After gaining possession, players must first play across the centerline before they can score a goal.
- Three goals with three goalkeepers stand back to back.
- Different size goals (large goal, junior size, mini goal) with different points system.
- Supplemental game: handball –headers (goals scored with the head only).

### Tips and suggestions

- Improved perceptual and action speed.
- Quick changeover from defense to offense, and vice versa.
- Crosses and back passes for the finish.
- Shots at the goal from all distances/rebounds.

# 13   Finally, a Few Suggestions

- As you introduce the new drills and plays, have patience and the necessary passion so your players will really comprehend and learn. Often it isn't easy to remember complex sequences and rules of play, and especially to apply them properly.
- When you choose drills and plays and their variations, always take into consideration the age and playing level of your players.
- Be creative and develop your own variations and personal training concepts. Our book will certainly help you.

We wish you success as you try out and diversify the various forms of training we introduced, and we hope that we were able to provide you with some valuable suggestions for your work as a trainer.

*Peter Schreiner & Norbert Elgert*

## Peter Schreiner

- UEFA-A licensee
- Founder and director of the German Institute for Youth Soccer
- Speaker at more than 200 seminars and conferences in more than 15 countries
- Presenter at BDFL (Federation of German Soccer Coaches) conferences
- Author of numerous articles in trade publications
- Co-owner, easy Sports software (*www.easy-sports-software.com*)

## Norbert Elgert

- Soccer coach, consultant in soccer education, speaker on motivation and team building
- Soccer pro for more than seven years (4 ½ years with FC Schalke 04)
- Coach for 21 years, of those one year as co-trainer in the 1st Division Bundesliga for FC Schalke 04, 15 years as head coach for U19 FC Schalke 04
- DFB Cup winner U19 FC Schalke 04, 2001/2002 season, 2004/2005 season
- German champion with U19 FC Schalke 04, 2005/2006 season, 2012 season
- Title winner U19 Bundesliga 2012 season
- Trainer, a.o., Mesut, Özil, Manuel Neuer, Benedikt Höwedes, Joel Matip, Julian Draxler, Mike Hanke.

## Author's Websites

*www.peter-schreiner-web.de*
*www.ifj96.de*
*www.soccer-coaches.com*
*www.en.easy-animation.com*
*www.sports-graphics.com*

## Literature/DVDs

### Books

Elgert, N. & Schreiner, P. (2010). *One Touch & Combination Play.* Essen: Institut für Jugendfußball

Hübscher, S. (2009). *Creative and Successful Wing Play.* Essen: Institut für Jugendfußball

### E-Books/Multimedia-Books

Wein, H. (2011). Online Book: *Small Sided Games for Develop Soccer Intelligence.* Essen: Institut für Jugendfußball

Peter, R. (2011). Online Book: *Pressing in Soccer, www.sports-graphics.com*

### DVDs/Online-DVDs (Institut für Jugendfußball, *www.ifj96.de*)

Elgert, N. & Schreiner, P. (2011). *The Art of Playing Attacking Soccer 1.* Essen: Institut für Jugendfußball

Elgert, N. & Schreiner, P. (2011). *The Art of Playing Attacking Soccer 2.* Essen: Institut für Jugendfußball

Elgert, N. & Schreiner, P. (2012). *The Art of Playing Attacking Soccer 3.* Essen: Institut für Jugendfußball

Wein, H. (2011). *Coaching Game Intelligence in Youth Football 1 und 2.* Essen: Institut für Jugendfußball

Wein, H. (2012). *Coaching Game Intelligence in Youth Football 3.* Essen: Institut für Jugendfußball

### Online Seminars (*www.soccer-coaches.com*)

Peter, R. (2012). *Zonal Defending 1-14.*

Peter, R. (2012). *Pressing in Soccer 1-4.*

## Picture Credits

| | |
|---|---|
| Coverdesign: | Andrea Brücher |
| Graphics: | Peter Schreiner |
| Layout: | Andrea Brücher |
| Copy Editing: | Michelle Demeter |
| Editing: | Sabine Carduck, Manuel Morschel |
| Photos: | firosportphotoGbr, Fromme+Ibing, Coesfelder Straße 207, 48249 Dülmen, Thinkstock (Coverbackground) |
| | dpa Picture-Alliance (pg. 5, 12/13, 19, 39, 46/47, 49, 81, 85, 90/91, 92/93, 109, 112/113, 124/125, 131, 156) |

The graphics in this book are created with the software easy Sports-Graphics. www.easy-sports-software.com